S0-BXZ-679

GLOBE FEARON

Survival Guide for Students

Globe
Fearon

Parsippany, New Jersey
www.pearsonlearning.com

Reviewers

Gary Duncan
Social Studies Teacher
Byrnedale Jr. High School
Toledo, Ohio

Richard Katz
Social Studies Department Supervisor
Asbury Park High School
Asbury Park, New Jersey

Kim Kozbial-Hess
Fourth Grade Teacher
Fall-Meyer Elementary School
Toledo, Ohio

Rod Martel
Licensed Psychologist
Chiron Middle School
Minneapolis, Minnesota

Gavin McGrath
Special Education Teacher
Asbury Park High School
Asbury Park, New Jersey

Kenneth J. Ratti
Science Department Chairperson
Vaca Peña Middle School
Vacaville, California

Carol Schneider
English Teacher
Crazy Horse School
Wanblee, South Dakota

Ken Simon
Social Studies Department Chairperson
Olson Middle School
Minneapolis, Minnesota

Project Editor: Lynn Kloss
Editor: Brian Hawkes
Editorial Assistant: Ryan Jones
Writer: Sandra Widener
Production Editor: Alan Dalgleish
Electronic Page Production: Mimi Raihl
Cover Design: Eve Adams

Grateful acknowledgment is made to The H. W. Wilson Company for its permission to reprint the selection "Harlem Renaissance" from *Readers' Guide to Periodical Literature*, 1989 Edition, Volume 49, page 866.

Copyright © 1997 by Globe Fearon, Inc. A Simon & Schuster company, One Lake Street, Upper Saddle River, New Jersey 07458. All rights reserved. No part of this book may be reproduced or transmitted in any form or by any means, electronic or mechanical, including photocopying, recording, or by any information storage and retrieval system, without permission in writing from the publisher.

Printed in the United States of America   6 7 8 9 10   01

ISBN 0-835-91932-3

CONTENTS

How to Use This Book

Everybody tells you to study. Your mother tells you to study every night. Your teacher reminds you to study for Friday's science test. Your coach says you have to study to stay on the team. Everybody tells you *to* study, but nobody tells you *how* to study. *Globe Fearon Survival Guide for Students* will help you.

Begin by taking the survey of your time management and study habits on page 1. Then read this book from beginning to end. This will give you an overview of how to study effectively and achieve success.

Then, the next time you're facing a new assignment or feeling that you simply can't get *everything* done, come back to this book. Look in the **Table of Contents** or the **Index** to find a specific topic, such as how to write a research paper or read a population map. Flip to the pages you need for a study tune-up.

These symbols will clue you in to what you'll find in this book.

 Clued In

The **Tips** are the heart of this book. Look for these when you need a quick strategy for completing a task.

CHAPTER CHECKUP Use the **Chapter Checkup** to review what you've learned or to be sure you've covered all of the bases.

The **Did You Know?** items offer interesting facts about time management and studying. Did you know?

The **Quotes** provide inspiration from successful people.

The **Quizzes** can help you think about how you are studying and managing your time. Quiz

Do The lists of **Do's and Don'ts** can Don't help you think about ways to complete assignments quickly and effectively.

Learning how to succeed is a life-long process. You might want to keep this book in a notebook and add your own survival tips as you discover them. You might also want to keep it on hand for the Reference section at the end of the book.

Remember that there are lots of different ways to study well. Try out the ideas in this book and decide which ones work for you.

Before You Begin

You probably have friends who are successful in school—even though they don't study. They cram for a test the night before, write a 10-page paper before breakfast, and never seem to take notes.

Believe it or not, these people probably need this book more than anyone! Whether you're a car mechanic or a college professor, you need to know how to manage your time and learn new skills. *Globe Fearon Survival Guide for Students* will show you how to do both of these things.

First, you'll learn how to organize your life, set goals, and manage your time. These are skills you will use when you plan projects for school, a party for a friend, or your career. They are skills you'll use to find time to do the things you *want* to do. They are also skills you'll use during the rest of your life.

Next, you will learn tips for school success. Taking notes, reading, doing research, writing, taking tests, and giving speeches are all skills you'll need in school and, probably, on the job. With a little practice, you'll find that your work will take less time because you'll have a system that works for you.

Last, you'll learn some tips for mastering your major subjects—language arts, math, science, and social studies. Other tips will help you improve your understanding and earn better grades in all of these areas.

Look at this book as a reference book, not as a textbook. Are you taking an essay test? Review the techniques for taking essay tests before you study. Do you have a big project? Review the tips for major projects.

Follow the tips in this book and you'll improve your performance in school. It's as simple as that. But these tips will also help you find time to play on a team, baby-sit for your little brother, succeed in a job, *and* find time for a social life!

What Are Your Strengths? What Are Your Weaknesses?

Take a survey of your habits to find out where you shine and where you could use some help. Once you know that, you can focus on the chapters that will help you the most.

Answer each question on a separate sheet of paper with the words *always, sometimes,* or *never.* Answer honestly. You won't be graded on the results. Let the answers help you make a plan for a successful future.

Unit 1: Organizing Your Time and Your Life

  1. Do you set goals and make a plan to reach them? (Chapter 1)
  2. Do you finish everything without scrambling at the last minute? (Chapter 2)

Unit 2: The Skills You Need to Succeed in School

  3. Do you remember what you study? (Chapter 3)
  4. Do you take well-organized notes that help you understand the subject? (Chapter 4)
  5. Do you understand and remember what you read? (Chapter 5)
  6. Can you use the library and the Internet to find what you need? (Chapter 6)
  7. Do you do as well on tests as you think you should? (Chapter 7)
  8. Do you write well and easily? (Chapter 8)
  9. Do you know how to write a research paper? (Chapter 9)
  10. Do you know how to prepare and give a speech? (Chapter 10)

Unit 3: Studying in the Subject Areas

  11. Do you know how to read and write the different forms of literature? (Chapter 11)
  12. Do you use problem-solving strategies in math? (Chapter 12)
  13. Do you use the scientific process? (Chapter 13)
  14. Do you know how to read and interpret maps? (Chapter 14)

Did you answer *always* to any of the questions? Congratulations! The chapter on these subjects will simply be a review for you. Did you answer *sometimes* or *never* to any questions? If so, you'll find suggestions for improving your skills in the chapters listed. Even if you are successful in an area, look for tips to make your work easier. You may find that you suddenly have more hours in your day—for fun.

UNIT 1

Organizing Your Time and Your Life

CHAPTER ONE

What You Need to Succeed

Success is hard to define. For some people, success means doing work they love. For others, success means earning a lot of money. Some people may think success means being happy. Others may think success means ending the school year on the honor roll.

However you define success, it doesn't just happen. *You* have to decide what you want and how to get there. You have to keep going until you succeed. The plan you make to reach your goals keeps you on track. The final element, keeping at it, is sometimes the hardest. Many people find it easy to list their goals and dreams. They find it easy to make a plan to reach them. But sticking with a plan? That's where things fall apart. In this chapter, you'll learn

- How to set goals.
- How to create to-do lists and set priorities.
- How to stick with something to get it done.

A Goal   +   A Plan   +   Sticking with It   =   Success

Setting Goals

Deciding what you want is also called *setting goals*. Setting goals is one of the best tools you have for success. A goal may be as simple as finishing your homework. It may also be as complex as deciding you want to be a veterinarian. Both of these goals are useful. They make it clear why you need to do certain things. To reach the goal of finishing your homework, you need to sit down and spend the time to do it. To become a veterinarian, you need to do well enough in school to get into and graduate from college.

How do you set goals? First, you realize that there are several kinds of goals you need to set.

- **Daily goals** such as finishing your math homework (A list of daily goals is also known as a *to-do list*.)

- **Short-term goals** such as getting a B average this year or saving enough money to go to a concert

- **Long-term goals** such as graduating from college with a degree in biology or buying a car

Simply choosing goals is not enough, though. You must also keep track of your goals. Some students keep lists of short- and long-term goals tacked to a bulletin board or wall where they can see them for inspiration. They then assign target dates for completing these goals so they can plan their time.

What's important about your goals is that they can keep you focused. If you understand that it's necessary to study algebra now to get into college, you'll feel better about finishing those math problems tonight.

Think about how long it might take you to reach each goal. Before you set target dates, consider your other responsibilities. Give yourself enough time to be successful.

Get into the habit of setting goals. You can start now.

1. **List your short-term goals.** You should be able to accomplish these in a few months or a year. Goals such as cleaning out your locker and finishing your social studies research paper are examples of short-term goals.

2. **List your long-term goals.** This list isn't set in stone. People often find that their goals change. People who have no goals, though, often find themselves drifting into something they never dreamed they would be doing—and aren't very happy about. Long-term goals can take a couple of years, or even a

" **Now, when I look back, I am grateful because hard work made me stronger and a more responsible person.** *"*

—June Kuramoto, musician

decade, to reach. Goals such as making the basketball team and saving money for college are examples of long-term goals.

Now, put today's date at the top of your lists. Again, set target dates to keep yourself focused. Put the lists of short- and long-term goals in a place that you see often. It's good to remember where you are heading.

Here's an example of how one student planned to achieve the long-term goals of joining the school basketball team and buying a stereo.

SETTING LONG-TERM GOALS

YOUR GOAL	EACH DAY	EACH WEEK	IN A MONTH	IN SIX MONTHS	IN ONE YEAR
To make the school basketball team.	I will shoot baskets for 45 minutes.	I will play in a pick-up game with my friends.	I will join a team at the local gym.	I will start to play with other members of the school team.	I will try out and make the school team.
To save enough money to buy a stereo.	I will figure out how much money I spend in a week.	I will set aside $2.00 a week for the stereo.	I will get a part-time job after school.	I will compare stereo prices.	I will buy the best stereo I can afford.

Making Lists and Setting Priorities

The To-Do List: A Daily Task

After you set goals, you need to manage your daily life so that you can meet these goals.

Lists of daily goals are also called *to-do lists*. As you complete things on your list, you can cross them off. This is satisfying. Daily goals are things you have to do, such as finishing homework assignments and doing chores around the house.

Daily goals also include things that you want to do, such as practicing your tennis serve for a half-hour. Because a major part of your to-do list will be schoolwork, keep the details of your homework assignments in an assignment book. (See Chapter 2 for more information about assignment and appointment calendars.) At the end of each day, make a new to-do list for the next day.

The Master List: Looking Ahead

You might find that it's helpful to make a master list of everything you need to get done or want to get done, from buying a birthday present to finding a summer job. The master list is a way to keep track of your responsibilities for a week or a month at a time. The only exception to this list is homework, which you should write in your assignment calendar. On your master list, write the date on which you want to accomplish each task, if you know it. Each day, scan the master list before you make your daily to-do list. Add whatever tasks you need to do to reach one or more of the goals on your master list. When you finish something, cross it off your master list.

Some people *really* know how to manage their time. Thomas Alva Edison, who invented the electric light bulb, set up a lab to create a new invention every 10 days. What's really remarkable is that he did it. In one four-year period, he produced 300 new inventions, or one every *five* days.

Setting Priorities

People who are serious about getting things done set priorities. You probably set priorities now without thinking about it. This means that you decide what needs to be done first, second, and last. If you really want to go to the basketball game, and you know you can't go unless you buy bread for your mother, your top priority will be going to the store.

Your master list will have items with different priorities. Each day, you will have items on your to-do list that have different priorities. You need to order these priorities so that you can be sure you finish the most important tasks. You can finish the less important ones if you have time.

Here is one way to look at setting priorities.

1. There are the things you have to get done, such as finishing homework that is due tomorrow.

2. There are the things you want to get done, such as shopping for new shoes.

3. There are the things you need to keep working on so you can finish them at a future date, such as beginning the research for a paper due in three weeks.

4. There are the things you need to get done to reach your long-term goals, such as finding a summer job in a field that interests you.

Now you need to mark your priorities on your lists in a way that helps you get them done.

Some people mark everything with a letter based on importance. An "A" is a "must do"; a "B" is a "would like to do"; a "C" is an "if I have time."

Some people write their to-do lists in order of importance. When they finish the first thing on the list, they cross it off and move on to the next thing.

Other people keep a to-do list with several sections. They do everything in the "must-do" part. Then they do the top things in the other sections.

Some people are well-organized enough just to look at their lists and know exactly what they need to do when. Think about what you learned about yourself in the quiz on page 1. Which of these choices fits you best?

> " Genius is one percent inspiration and ninety-nine percent perspiration. "
>
> —Thomas Alva Edison, inventor

This chart shows you how one student set her priorities.
Notice that she also scheduled time for long-term projects.

MASTER LIST FOR THE WEEK OF 10/15/98

PRIORITY	DUE DATE	LEVEL OF PRIORITY
Revise English paper	10/30	B
Go to a movie with friends	none	B
Study for History exam	10/22	A
Play basketball	none	C
Buy Mom a birthday gift	10/16	A
Go to Bob's party	10/22	C

Clued In

Ten Tips for Sticking with It

Now comes the hard part. How do you force yourself to turn off the TV or video game and get to work? Here are some tips. Start by using one tip at a time. If it works for you, keep doing it. Then try another tip.

- Break a big job into small jobs. Then start one of the small jobs.

- Set aside a time each day (the same time, if you can manage it) for doing the work. Make it a reasonable block of time (20 minutes) that you know you always have free or can make free.

Did you know?

Have you ever used the excuse that the dog ate your homework? In the case of the author John Steinbeck, it was true. His dog ate half of the pages on which the original *Of Mice and Men* was written.

- If you're working on something you don't like, start by spending only 10 minutes at a time on it. You can do anything for 10 minutes. Then take a break or study something else before you go back to it.

- Don't waste time. When it's time to work, start working. Get something accomplished right away.

- Make an agreement with a friend that you'll call each other at a certain time to study. Then do it.

- Every day, when you finish, reward yourself for sticking with it. Go running. Watch a TV show. Do something you enjoy. Do something for *you*!

- Record your progress. Draw a chart and record the time you spend working every day. If you don't do anything, write 0. Writing things down makes them real.

- Are you losing interest? Do you feel like you're stuck? Talk to a teacher, a friend, or a parent. Tell the person what you've done and what you need to do. You'll be impressed with what you've done, and he or she might have some ideas for next steps.

- If you're stuck, you can also try working on a different part of the project, or looking at it in a different way.

- Don't allow yourself to be distracted. Let that phone ring.

The Path to Success

As you can see, just *having* goals isn't enough. Once you set a goal, come up with a plan to reach that goal. Start a master list. Make a to-do list. Organize both of these lists by importance. Now that you've done this, you're on the path to success.

> **"You've got to persevere. Stick with it—that's the main thing."**
> —Gloria Estefan, singer

CHAPTER CHECKUP

Sit down with a pencil and a piece of paper. For every question you can answer "yes," write a check on a separate sheet of paper.

✓ Do you rarely use excuses for not getting things done—because you get them done?

✓ Do you make daily to-do lists?

✓ Do you set long-term goals?

✓ Do you set short-term goals?

✓ Do you use a master list?

✓ Do you set priorities and get your high-priority activities done?

✓ Do you usually get up from studying having accomplished everything you planned?

✓ Are you able to stick with a project or assignment and finish it?

Now, count up your checks. How many do you have? If you have 8, you're likely to get what you want. If you have between 5 and 7, try some of the tips in this chapter. You'll be pleased at how much closer you can get to your goals. If you have 4 or fewer checks, take a serious look at your habits. You need to take charge and begin getting things done.

Now think about what you learned in this chapter.

1. Which three tips worked best for you?

2. How did these tips help you?

CHAPTER TWO

Tips for Organizing Your Time

There's no better feeling than knowing exactly how and when you're going to get something done. People who have trouble organizing their time wish for a magic wand that will put everything in order. Well, that's unlikely to happen, but you can train yourself to get things done. How? This chapter offers help in

- Finding more hours in the day.
- Putting together a fool-proof assignment book.
- Making the most of your study time.
- Putting your body clock to work for you.
- Keeping a time log to sharpen your organizational skills.

Does This Happen to You?

If you find yourself answering "yes" to these questions, it's time to try some new ways of organizing your time.

- Do you find yourself missing due dates for assignments?
- Are you often in a last-minute panic because you forget an assignment?
- Do you turn in work you're not proud of because you don't leave yourself enough time to do it right?
- Are you often late for class or to meet friends for appointments?
- Do you miss appointments because you forget about them?

Most people will probably answer "yes" to at least some of these questions. Very few people manage their time well. But if you're telling yourself that it's not your fault and there are just not enough hours in the day, it's time for the next exercise.

Real-Life Help: Where Does Your Time Go?

How do you spend your time? Most people are surprised to find out what they actually do during a day. For at least a day, carry a notebook with you wherever you go. Make sure you wear a watch. From the moment you get up to the moment you go to bed, write down everything you do and how long it takes.

At the end of the day, take a look at your list. Here are some questions to ask yourself.

- Where have I wasted time? (Don't forget time you spend waiting for something—you can use that time, too.)

- How could I do what I do more efficiently?

Clued In

Finding More Hours in the Day

Here are some tips for making your time count.

- Use your to-do list to give you the feeling that you're on top of your life.

- Use the bits of time you might waste. Look at the list of where you spend your time. You'll probably find 5 minutes here and 10 minutes there you can spend on homework. Use it.

- Use space efficiently—it will help you use time efficiently. For example, if you have two errands to do that are close to each other, schedule them together.

- Combine tasks. You can have a snack while you talk on the phone.

- Assemble everything you need before you start a job. If you spend 20 minutes looking for a stapler, you waste 20 minutes.

- Do things right away that will take more effort to do later. For example, if you don't put your clothes away, they'll get wrinkled and you'll have to iron them, which takes more time.

- If you find it impossible to be on time, try this. Note how late you are most times. For example, if you're usually 15 minutes late for an appointment, make it a habit to leave 15 minutes earlier—for every appointment. Being on time can make you feel less flustered—and it's a good way to impress people.

- This sounds silly, but it really helps some people: Set your clock and watch ahead by 3 minutes. Even if you can't fool yourself, it may keep you aware of exactly what time it is.

- Keep your assignment and appointment calendar with you. When you make an appointment, write it down that minute.

The first known mechanical clock was made by the Chinese imperial tutor Su Sing in 1088. The clock was 30 feet high and was powered by running water.

The Never-Fail Assignment and Appointment Calendar

If organizing your class work and your free time is a problem, try keeping an assignment calendar.

> **I must govern the clock, not be governed by it.**
>
> —Golda Meir,
> former prime minister of Israel

1. Get a calendar that you can keep with you at all times. It should have spaces that are large enough for you to write what you need to do each day. Some students prefer to make their own calendar pages and put them into a special section in their notebooks. Others buy an appointment book that fits into a three-ring notebook. You can find organizers at office supply stores and discount stores. Your school may also offer them.

2. When you get an assignment or a test date, immediately write it in your calendar under the day it is due. Write the subject and what the assignment is. If it's a big assignment or a major test, you may want to write it in red.

3. If it's something you need to start long before it's due, such as a big project, break the task into pieces. Write the smaller pieces as assignments you'll complete one by one. Then you'll have enough time to get the whole project done.

APPOINTMENT CALENDAR FOR NOVEMBER

MONDAY	TUESDAY	WEDNESDAY	THURSDAY	FRIDAY	SATURDAY	SUNDAY
1	2	3	4	5 finish 1st draft of history paper	6 movie with Marie—8pm	7
8 basketball tryouts—3:30	9	10	11	12	13	14 Dad's birthday
15	16	17 Language Arts test	18	19 history paper due	20	21
22	23	24	25 Thanksgiving	26	27	28
29	30					

4. Write in your calendar every date that's important to you. This could be basketball practice, a baby-sitting job, or a date that your dad has asked you to pick up your little sister from school. This calendar will help you keep all of your dates organized and in one place.

A Few Useful Tips about Time and Studying

Researchers have tried to find out the most effective length of time to study. Their conclusion: Study in 20-minute blocks. The first 10 minutes and the last 10 minutes of studying are the most productive, so put those minutes together. After that, take a 10-minute break. Have a snack. Phone a friend. Do 20 pushups. When you are able to focus again, work another 20 minutes. Need more motivation to work this way? Students who studied for five half-hour sessions did 10 percent better on tests than those who studied 2½ hours at one time.

Another odd fact is that you can save time by spending it. By using the tips in "Finding More Hours in the Day" in this chapter, you'll spend some time planning. When you do that, though, you won't waste as much time later.

If you really can't concentrate when you study, you're wasting your time. Do something else for 15 minutes. Come back fresh and try again.

Have you ever been "in the groove"? When you're really involved in something, like shooting baskets, you probably lose track of time. How can you achieve this when you're studying? Become actively interested in what you're learning. Set yourself a challenge. It may seem strange, but pushing yourself to learn more can keep you focused.

Some people have *no* trouble studying. Adragon Eastwood De Mello graduated from the University of California in Santa Cruz in 1988 with a degree in mathematics. He was 11 years old.

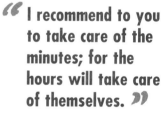

❝ I recommend to you to take care of the minutes; for the hours will take care of themselves. ❞

—Lord Chesterfield, political leader

When Are You Brilliant?

Do you know the best time for you to do schoolwork? Answering the questions below should show you when you're at your best. That's when you should study. To answer these questions, think about how you feel when you're studying—and how you feel the rest of the time. You might plan to do something that doesn't take your full attention—like raking the leaves—when you're less alert.

- When do you feel most wide awake?

- When do you feel most creative?

- At what time of the day do you concentrate best?

- Do you have the most trouble staying awake in the afternoon, late at night, or early in the morning?

Keep a Time Log

If you have trouble answering these questions, keep a time log for about a week. In the log, note when you feel sleepy and when you feel energetic. Write when you go to sleep and when you wake up. At the end of the week, look at what you wrote. Note when you're most awake. Try to do the things that require careful attention then, like studying.

Also look at the number of hours you sleep. If you're sleeping fewer than 7 or 8 hours a night, you might be dragging during the day. Find ways to add some hours of sleep. You'll be able to get more done during the day if you're well rested.

CHAPTER CHECKUP

To see how well you organize your time, keep a time log for three days. As you use the following tips, check them. At the end of the three days, notice what you didn't check. Go back to the chapter and see if adding those tips helps you use your time better.

✓ I make and keep a to-do list.

✓ I use the little bits of time "wasted" during the day.

✓ I have everything I need when I start a job.

✓ I do things right away if they will take more effort to do later.

✓ I combine tasks when I can.

✓ I break up big assignments by scheduling a little time each day to work on them.

✓ I study during the time of day that I'm most awake.

✓ I study in 20-minute blocks.

✓ I'm on time for appointments and for class.

✓ I keep my personal appointments and school assignments together so that I don't forget anything.

✓ I balance my school and personal appointments so that I can do both well.

Now think about what you learned in this chapter.

1. What kind of calendar have you decided to use for your personal and school appointments?

2. When is the best time for you to do tasks that require your full attention?

UNIT 2

The Skills You Need to Succeed in School

CHAPTER THREE

Studying Better

As you learn how to study effectively, you'll spend less time studying and you'll get better results. You'll find that the entire process can be efficient—and painless. You'll also find how to be successful in school—and have a social life.

This chapter offers you tips for putting your study time to work for *you*, including

- Using a studying technique that works.
- Making a plan to study effectively.
- Finding a good place to study.
- Identifying your study style and making it work for you.
- Using the Index Card Solution.
- Using memory tricks.
- Handling long-term projects.
- Handling group projects.
- Organizing a study group.
- Keeping track of your studies.

What You Must Know

For every assignment, or for anything you plan to do, keep these two points in mind.

- **Know the point of the assignment.** If you start your homework without understanding why you're doing it, you're wasting time. Think for a minute. Why did the teacher assign this? What did he or she want you to learn?
- **Know what you want to accomplish.** What do you want to study today? The more specific you are, the better. For example, you might want to understand a verb tense in French. Review your to-do list and your assignment book before you start studying. At the end of the day, you'll have the satisfaction of knowing that you've done what you planned.

What to Do When You Sit Down

No matter what you're studying, the following technique will help you learn it better. You can adapt the technique to reading a novel, studying biology, or learning math. Think of a study session as having three parts.

Overview: The Appetizer

Don't just plunge in. First, think about what the point of the assignment is, and what you're trying to accomplish. Next, look through the material. Notice headings and main points, or just familiarize yourself with the work before you start it. You'll be amazed at how much faster you'll finish your homework when you know what's coming. Also, think about what you're about to do and how it relates to what you've already done in the class.

> " Every hurdle we jump strengthens and prepares us for the next one, (and shows us that) we're already on the way to success. "
>
> —Benjamin Carson, neurosurgeon

Assignment: The Main Course

Work until you understand what the teacher wants you to learn. In most subjects, it doesn't make sense to memorize lots of little details. It bogs you down and confuses you. Figure out the main points and learn them. Depending on the topic, you might do this by reading, reviewing lab notes, or working on math problems.

Work in 20-minute blocks, with short breaks between blocks, until you know what you need to know. With most assignments, taking notes will help. Based on your learning style, you might want to do this in diagrams, written notes, or notes that you repeat to yourself out loud. (See "The Index Card Solution" in this chapter for suggestions for taking effective notes.)

Review: The Dessert

Studying should have a satisfying end. Check that you really learned what you think you learned. You also need to remember the information for more than 5 minutes. You can do this by reviewing.

There are several ways to review. One way is to read through your notes quickly, making sure you understand them. Another way is to sit down and imagine you're the teacher. What questions would you ask if you were planning to give a quiz? Write the questions. Then answer them. A third way to review is to write a summary of what you've just learned. However you do it, it's satisfying to realize that you really do understand your assignment.

What Tools Do You Need?

If you need a calculator and can't find one, you'll waste valuable time. Keep everything you need where you study. If you study both at home and school, consider having two sets of studying tools: one that stays in your backpack and another that stays at home. Look over the following list and check what you need. Then make sure you have everything handy.

✓ writing paper	✓ pencils
✓ pens	✓ eraser
✓ calculator	✓ ruler
✓ colored pencils	✓ stapler
✓ tape	✓ glue
✓ paper clips	✓ pencil sharpener
✓ index cards	✓ dictionary

Clued In

Heloise's Tips for Organizing a Drawer

Heloise, who is famous for her "Hints From Heloise" newspaper column and books, has spent her life inventing organizing tips. Here's her suggestion for organizing a drawer.

First, take everything out of the main drawer in your desk. Next, wipe out the drawer. Now start putting things back—but do it carefully. What do you use every day? Don't put more than one of anything in, unless you use more than one of this item in the drawer. (Pencils and pens are an exception. Having extras of these can save you time.)

Now, look at everything that's left. Put what you might need for a specific project in another, less convenient, drawer. Put everything else in a bag. Store it. You'll probably find that you'll never look in the bag again. As Heloise says, "What you can do without, you don't need."

Where to Study?

There's no rule that says you must sit up straight, use your desk, and turn off the TV. You may be at your best studying in bed propped up by a pillow while you read *The Adventures of Huckleberry Finn*.

Chances are, though, that you're more likely to fall asleep than concentrate when you're in bed. You'll probably also admit that when the TV's on, your attention wanders. Research shows that students who sit at a desk and who don't watch TV or listen to distracting music study more effectively than those who have one eye on the TV. Students who work with fewer distractions learn faster and remember more.

Not all your studying has to be done in your room. Here are some other possibilities.

- your school library

- your town library or a local college library

- your living room or basement

- your kitchen table

Make your study spot comfortable. Make it inviting. Use a chair that doesn't hurt your back. Use a light that's bright enough so you don't have to peer into the book. Keep your work area neat. It's amazing how much better you'll feel when the space around you is organized.

What's Your Study Style?

People learn best in different ways. If you put your style to work for you, studying will be easier. What's your style—listening, seeing, or doing?

- **Listening.** Some people are *auditory learners*—they remember best what they hear. If someone describes a complicated process, they remember every detail. If listening is your style, try tape-recording your notes. Then play them back.

- **Seeing.** Other people are *visual learners*. They remember diagrams, pictures, and the location of words on a page. If this is your style, arrange your notes to be visually attractive. Use graphic organizers like idea maps or diagrams to help you remember ideas.

- **Doing.** Some people learn best by *doing things*. They can listen to directions for putting together an engine and not be able to do any of the parts. But give these people the chance to do it—to use their hands to learn—and they're stars. If doing is your style, try a hands-on approach. Act it out. Try it yourself.

The Index Card Solution

There's only one corner of the universe you can be certain of improving, and that's your own self.

—Aldous Huxley, writer

Invest in a set of multicolored index cards. Assign a color to each class. These cards can be your lifeline. Every time you study, write each main idea or critical concept on a card. These cards will help you discipline yourself to concentrate on important ideas, because you only have room to put one idea on each card. You can use them like flash cards. Write the concept on one side. On the other side, list what it is and why it's important.

Now, here's the great part. Take the cards with you and study when you're stuck doing nothing. When you're waiting in line for something, take out the cards and get to work. That's studying you won't have to do later. When you're sure you know the idea on a card, put it in another pile for later review. While your friends are sitting at their desks trying to remember the important facts about a World War II battle, you'll have learned them already.

These cards will also come in handy when you study for tests. A few days before a test, get out all the cards for the course and start reviewing them. That should be most of what you have to do to get ready for the test.

Clued In

Memory Tricks

Tricks can help you remember things that you have to memorize, not reason your way through. Here are some tricks to help.

- **Use acronyms.** Make up an acronym (the first letters spell a word) to remind you of something. For example, the first letters of the Great Lakes spell HOMES—Huron, Ontario, Michigan, Erie, and Superior.

- **Make up a rhyme.** "In fourteen hundred and ninety two, Columbus sailed the ocean blue." Your rhyme doesn't have to make sense. You don't have to tell it to anyone. You just have to be able to remember it.

- **Make associations.** Associate a memorable characteristic with something you know well. You might remember word definitions this way. For example, if you associate the word

Did you know ?

Gon Yangling of China needs no memory tricks. He has memorized more than 15,000 telephone numbers of people in Harbin, China.

saccharine with a person at school who is falsely sweet, you'll remember the meaning of the word.

- **Make up a silly story.** If you have to remember a series of objects, places, and people, make up a silly story that includes them all. The story will help you remember the objects.

- **Use acrostics.** An acrostic is a puzzle in which the first letter of each word is a stand-in for a whole word, or sometimes just for the letter itself. You may remember "Every Good Boy Does Fine" from music classes when you tried to memorize the lines on the treble clef—EGBDF.

- **Break it up.** Do you have a long list of numbers or letters, or a long formula to memorize? Break it up into several short pieces instead of one long one: 398726254 can become 398 726 254.

- **Draw a mind picture.** Some people (visual learners, for example) find that creating a picture helps them remember. For example, you might be able to remember a map of where an important event occurred, such as the journeys along the Oregon Trail. You can pull up that map from your memory and remember the details. Other people find it handy to remember a drawing they made of a concept or a set of ideas. They can remember the diagram with the information on it.

- **Recite it.** When you say something aloud, you can often organize it in a way that you can remember later.

- **Concentrate.** Think about something you remember easily. You probably remember it because it was important to you. You *made* yourself remember it. When you have to remember something, concentrate. Tell yourself that it is important, and tell yourself that you *will* remember it. You probably will.

Facing a Long-Term Project?

Do you have one of these two reactions to a long-term project?

1. Your heart sinks. Immediately, you think you'll never be able to get it done. The topic is huge. It looks hopeless.

2. You grin. It's not due until the end of the semester? You'll worry about it then.

As you've probably guessed, you're headed for trouble if you react in either of these ways. Managing long-term projects can be done, however. What's more, a project can even be something you look forward to, if you choose something you want to study.

Clued In

Here are some tips for getting that long-term project done—and enjoying it.

- **Choose something you want to study.** Most long-term projects involve some choice. Choose something you want to know more about. The topic should be worth long-term study and yet not be too big or too small to be practical.

- **Break the work into pieces.** A long-term project can seem like an unclimbable mountain unless you break down the work. You might not be able to write a 20-page paper tomorrow, but you can go to the library to find the books that might help you.

- **Plan a schedule.** Work backward from the due date. Figure out the major tasks, then space them so you're not rushing at the last minute. When you have a schedule, transfer it to your assignment book. Plan a little extra time at the end for unexpected problems, such as results you didn't expect.

- **Consider these assignments as important as any other.** It may be easy to put them off now, but you'll pay later. If you get behind, don't give up. Catch up. You're going to have to do it anyway, so do it now.

Handling Group Projects

Group projects can be fun and challenging—or frustrating. Sometimes the grade reflects one member's laziness. One thing to keep in mind is that group projects are often designed with that in mind. Teachers may want to challenge a student who's not working. Peer pressure can sometimes do that, if a bad grade will affect the entire group.

Many of the same tips for major projects apply to group projects. For example, break down the project into smaller tasks. Then schedule these smaller tasks. Here are some tips for managing a group project.

- **Assign a project manager.** This person may have fewer day-to-day assignments. That way, the manager can focus on keeping track of everything. This person is the key to a

" **A journey of a thousand miles must begin with a single step.** "

—Lao-Tzu, philosopher

successful group. He or she should have the "people skills" to convince others to do what has to be done.

- **Play to strengths.** People have interests and skills in different areas. One might be an artist who can work on a presentation. Another might be someone who is a strong public speaker. Use these skills.

- **Keep on track.** Have weekly meetings to make sure work is getting done and everyone is working toward the same goal.

- **Solve little problems before they become big ones.** If things aren't getting done, have a group meeting and discuss problems. The project manager has the most important role here. He or she has to help the group find a solution and make sure the agreed solution is acted upon.

Is a Study Group for You?

Study groups can help you. You have built-in motivation and built-in peer pressure. Groups can be fun, too. Here are some tips for starting a study group.

- **Be careful whom you ask.** You don't want to be the only hard-working person in the group. You'll feel resentful that you're doing all of the work. Choose people who have similar work habits, are willing to spend time working, and can be counted on.

- **Make the group a reasonable size.** Two is probably too small; eight is too big. Keep it small enough so people feel responsible and large enough so you can spread out the work. Three to five people is usually a good size for a group.

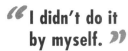

" I didn't do it by myself. "

—Emmitt Smith,
athlete

- **Do a trial run.** You or a friend may think the idea sounds good, but want to see how it works. Hold a no-commitments session. That way you might be able to interest others.

- **Assign a manager.** You need a manager or a rotating manager. This person should make sure that people know the rules, show up, do the work, and cover everything. This person's only job in the study group might be as manager.

People set up study groups in different ways. Most study groups meet weekly. Some assign members to do detailed reviews of what's happened in a specific class. Others go over their classes in order, with members offering their opinions about the most important areas covered during the last week, and making sure they understand the concepts. Some of these groups assign different members to take notes about what the group discusses and distribute the notes to everyone.

One of the best ways to use study groups is to review for tests. Have everyone make up a sample test for each class. Each test should cover the most important points of the material. Then put the questions together and have everyone take the tests and discuss the answers.

Clued In

Tips for Sticking With It

One of the best things you can do when you're studying is to stick with it. If you find yourself falling behind, schedule some extra time to catch up—immediately. Here are some other ways to keep on track as the school year continues.

- **Continually add to and review your index cards.** As you learn what's on a card, put it aside. By the end of the semester, you should have all of the main points in the class written on index cards.

- **Schedule weekly review sessions.** Review what you learn every week. Then look at what you've done so far in the semester. Use all your index cards for this, starting with the ones you've already learned. If you've forgotten things you thought you knew, add these cards back into the pile.

- **If you miss classes, catch up.** Borrow the notes from a student who takes good notes.

- **If you can't understand something, get help.** In many classes, learning builds on learning. You have to understand one idea before you can learn the next.

CHAPTER CHECKUP

How well do you study? Review this chapter using the techniques you've learned. Then answer these questions.

- ✓ What are two things you should know when you sit down to study?
- ✓ Describe the three parts of a study session.
- ✓ What does research show about the best place to study?
- ✓ What are the three study styles?
- ✓ Describe the Index Card Solution.
- ✓ Name five memory tricks.
- ✓ What are three tips for doing well on a long-term project?
- ✓ Name three ways to handle a group project successfully.
- ✓ What are the steps for starting a study group?

Now think about what you learned in this chapter.

1. What is your study style?
2. How can you make your study style work for you?

CHAPTER FOUR

Study Skills for Every Class

You can slink into class, slouch into your seat, and stare at your desk. Probably no one will stop you. What a boring way to spend an hour. Of course, there is another way. You can listen. Become interested. You'll have a better time than if you sit there wishing the class were over. Here are some tips for learning more and for participating in ways that may improve your grade. In this chapter, you'll learn

- How to get the most out of class.

- How to improve your listening skills.

- How to "read" your teacher.

- Three approaches to note taking.

- Note-taking do's and don'ts.

Show Up Ready to Learn

Teachers spend their class time teaching you what you should know. They may give you assignments that take hours outside of class, but there are only so many hours of class time. How do you make that time count for you?

- Come to class prepared. It sounds simple, and it is.

- If you will need supplies during class, such as books or a calculator, bring them.

- If you have reading to do before the class, do it.

- If you have an assignment due, finish it and bring it in on time.

Why should you be prepared? If you know what to expect, you'll be better able to understand what's happening. Here's the other reason you should be prepared. Many teachers check to see if you're prepared. They call on you for answers, give quizzes, and expect you to discuss the material. If you know what's going on, this will be a breeze.

Getting the Most Out of Time in Class

Once you're in class, the most important thing is to be an active learner. That means taking notes. (See "Note Taking to Get Great Grades" in this chapter for more information.) It also means participating in class. Most teachers base students' grades at least in part on class participation.

How can you be an active learner? Here are some things to do, and some other things to avoid.

✓ Do

1. Ask questions when you don't understand something. If you've done the work, your questions will show it. They'll probably be questions other students have, too.

2. Volunteer to answer questions.

3. Write your questions as they occur to you if you're nervous about speaking up. Check them off when they're answered. Then ask the questions that are left.

4. Comment only when you can add to the discussion.

⊗ Don't

1. Answer questions only when the teacher calls on you. Instead, volunteer answers.

2. Talk only to hear yourself talk. Instead, be sure you have something to contribute to the discussion.

3. Try to cover up if you don't know an answer. Instead, if you don't know an answer, say so. Don't try to be funny or talk about something unrelated. It won't work.

4. Interrupt when someone else is speaking. Instead, listen respectfully to your teacher and to the other students in the class.

Quiz

How Well Do You Listen?

Find out how well you really listen by answering these questions.

✓ Do you often have to ask people to repeat things?

✓ Do you often think of the next thing you want to say while someone else is still talking?

✓ Do you interrupt to ask a question that someone is answering?

✓ Do you daydream while you listen, or doodle in your notepad instead of taking notes?

✓ Do you look away from the person who is talking?

If you answered yes to 3 or more questions, you need a listening skills tune-up.

Listening Skills Tune-up

How can you become a better listener? Try using some of these hints to improve how much you learn, understand, and remember. You could start with one of these techniques and add one each day. At the end of the week, you'll be an active listener.

- **Focus.** Put your attention—all your attention—on the person speaking. Look at him or her. If you find yourself wandering, pull yourself back.

- **Get it the first time.** For one day, try your hardest not to ask people to repeat things. Concentrate so you hear the information the first time.

- **Don't interrupt.** Practice not finishing sentences for others or interrupting before they're finished. What they're saying may not be what you expect to hear.

- **Don't do anything else.** When someone talks to you, stop watching TV. Stop doing whatever it is you're doing (unless you're taking notes on what you're hearing). You'll remember more.

Clued In

How to "Read" Your Teacher

Speakers, whether they're teachers or anyone else, give you clues to what they think is important. Here are some tips. See how many your teachers use. Good speakers often

- Repeat important ideas.

- Use their voice to emphasize important ideas.

- Signal importance with phrases such as "There are three critical . . .," "The most important thing to remember is . . .," or the ever-popular, "You will be tested on . . ."

- Write important points on the board.

- Use nonverbal clues, such as using their fingers to list ideas or gesturing dramatically.

Note Taking to Get Great Grades

There are several ways to take notes. All of them have some things in common, though. (See "Note-Taking Do's and Don'ts" on page 30 of this chapter.) Here is an overview of some of the most popular ways to take notes.

Did you know?

According to *Isaac Asimov's Book of Facts,* the most successful textbook writer of all time was Euclid, who wrote a geometry textbook in 300 B.C. Until recently, when people studied geometry, they said, "I studied my Euclid."

Some students find a style and use it for all their classes. Other students prefer to match a style of note taking to a class. For example, one teacher may speak in a carefully organized way that allows you to outline the class. Another teacher may prefer to discuss several sides of an issue. In that case, it might make sense to use an idea map. (See "Idea Mapping" below for more information.)

Outlining

You may already know how to outline. You begin with the Roman numeral *I* that lists the first main idea. Then you add capital letters for major points. You follow these with Arabic numerals for details. If you need even more detail, you add lower-case letters. Outlined notes look like this.

I. African Americans move to cities after World War II

    A. What happens to African Americans in cities?

        1. Find bad treatment

           a. discrimination

           b. poor housing

In an outline format, it's easy to tell which points are most important. Experienced students often use outlining.

Main Points

Here's a different form of outlining. It is difficult for many students to concentrate on what the teacher is saying and write a perfect outline at the same time. Instead, write a main idea the teacher is discussing. Underline it. Then, under that, indent the next lines. Write the important things the teacher talks about relating to that topic. If you hear things you think are particularly important, or that the teacher emphasizes, underline them. When the teacher begins another main point or topic, skip a line and start again. The outline for the topic above might look something like this.

African Americans move to cities after WW2

    What happened after the move? Bad treatment. Discrimination. Poor housing.

Idea Mapping

This way of taking notes appeals to those who learn best by seeing. It's also a good method when teachers seem to skip around. What you're doing is trying to create a map that shows relationships among ideas.

"Education is when you read the fine print; experience is what you get when you don't."
—Pete Seeger, folk singer

Start by writing the main idea in the center of the paper. Then circle it. As you hear ideas that are related to the main idea, write them around the circled main idea. When you hear important details about the secondary ideas, write them and attach them to the secondary idea. The notes written above might look like this.

"Try to find something that works and stay with it. ")

—Robb Sagendorph,
economist

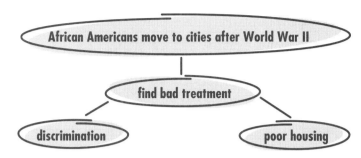

For people who remember best by seeing, a map like this can be a visual aid. These people often find they can remember where the circles were on the page. That helps them remember what was in each circle.

Note-Taking Do's and Don'ts

Here are a few guidelines to help you take effective notes.

✓ Do

1. Write the date and the topic of the class at the top of all notes. Number the pages.

2. Take notes on lined, three-hole-punched paper.

3. Leave about a third of the space on the page blank, either on the bottom or the side. Use that space to add information later.

4. Write only main points and ideas.

5. Use abbreviations. Create your own shorthand.

6. Underline for emphasis.

⊗ Don't

1. Write every word and detail you hear. You'll spend so much time writing, you'll lose track of what the teacher is saying.

2. Tape-record every class. Instead, sharpen your listening and note-taking skills.

3. Erase. Instead, draw a line through things you mis-heard. That saves what you wrote in case you were right the first time. It also takes less time than erasing.

4. Write sloppily. You won't understand what you wrote.

5. Give up if you get behind. Instead, wait until you hear another main point, and jump in again. Later, you can ask a friend or the teacher for the information you missed.

6. Doodle. It's easy to get so involved with doodling that you miss something important. Instead of doodling, practice the art of listening.

CHAPTER CHECKUP

Review a day's classes. Then check this list. How many of these things did you do?

✓ Did you bring the right supplies to class?

✓ Did you make the most of class once you were there?

✓ Did you ask questions when you didn't understand something?

✓ Did you add to the discussion in class?

✓ Did you focus when the teacher was speaking?

✓ Did you notice your teacher's signals: using clue words, repeating important ideas, and writing important points on the board?

✓ Did you use a way of taking notes that will help you remember the most important things the teacher said to the class—either outlining, writing the main points, or idea mapping?

✓ When you were taking notes, did you leave part of the space on each page blank?

✓ Did you use abbreviations and create your own shorthand?

✓ Did you take care to keep up, and to get help if you needed it?

If you checked 10 of the items above, you're getting the most from class. Any fewer and you need to go back and review the chapter.

Now think about what you learned in this chapter.

1. Make a list of the listening skills you used in one of your classes today.

2. Which method of note taking do you prefer?

3. Why do you prefer this method?

CHAPTER FIVE

Get More Out of Reading

To be successful at school, you need to read well. That's pretty obvious. Much of what you learn both in school and outside of school, you learn through books. Your job, then, is to become an effective reader. Once you do that, you will read books more quickly and remember more.

In this chapter, you'll learn

- When to vary the way you read.

- How to be an active reader.

- Whether you should speed read.

- How to get rid of bad reading habits.

- How to use your learning style to get the most out of reading.

- How to increase your vocabulary.

Are You Book Smart?

See if you can match the following with the correct response.

1. What kind of animal is the main character in *The Call of the Wild*?

2. What is the name of the first book in *The Chronicles of Narnia* series by C. S. Lewis?

3. Where does the family live in *The Little House in the Big Woods*?

4. What is the name of the main character in *The Hobbit* by J. R. R. Tolkien?

5. Where is the family stranded in *The Swiss Family Robinson*?

a. *The Lion, the Witch, and the Wardrobe*

b. on the American prairie

c. on a deserted island

d. Bilbo Baggins

e. a sled dog

(Answers are on page 39.)

> **Of all people's diverse tools, undoubtedly the most astonishing are their books.**
> —Jorge Luis Borges,
> writer

The Kinds of Reading

You already read in many different ways. You read newspaper sports scores quickly, skimming to learn about a specific team. You read instructions for assembling a bike carefully so you'll go forward, not backward. You read novels that you choose at the pace at which you'll best enjoy the book.

There are different kinds of reading at school, too. Some are specific, such as reading literature and science books. You'll learn more about these skills in later chapters in this book. Here are the three basic ways that you'll need to read to succeed in school.

"I always begin at the left with the opening word of the sentence and read toward the right and I recommend this method."

—James Thurber, humorist

- **Skimming.** When you skim a book, you take a quick look to see what it contains. You look at the table of contents and chapter headings. You look for something specific. For example, you may be writing a paper about whales and want to find information about what they eat. You can skim to learn that.

- **Careful reading.** When you read textbooks, it's usually best to read carefully. This kind of reading helps you learn most effectively. You read for concepts, for main ideas, and for broad understanding. A careful reader is an active reader; see "Active Reading and Textbooks" on page 34.

- **Deep reading.** When you have to learn every detail, you'll probably read deeply. You read deeply most often when you're following a complicated process in mathematics, or when you're trying to assemble something from instructions. You know it is important to know every bit of information.

Active Reading

What's the last thing you read that you remember? What's the last thing you read that you don't remember? Most likely, what you remember is something you wanted to read. You focused on the book or article. Maybe you argued mentally with the author or wondered what the next point would be. You were an active reader.

Now think about something you don't remember reading. You knew you had to read this material, but you daydreamed. You thought about how long it would be until you finished. This is passive reading, and it's frustrating. While you may not like some of the reading you have to do, you can read more effectively if you read actively.

Active Reading and Textbooks

How can you actively read your textbooks?

- **Preview.** If you know what's coming, you're more likely to be prepared for it and absorb it. Here's how to preview.

  First, look at the whole book quickly by skimming the table of contents. The table of contents outlines the book. It will also show you how the material is organized.

  Now look at the chapter or the section you're reading. Read the headings and subheadings. Read the introduction and conclusion to the chapter. Previewing gives you a good idea of what you're going to read.

- **Ask questions.** If you're active, you're thinking. As you preview, jot down the questions that come to mind when you look at the chapter headings. What do you want to know? What don't you understand? You'll answer your questions later.

  If you think that this sounds like too much trouble, think again. Writing your questions can also help you review for tests. You may even find that your questions will show up on a test.

- **Break down your reading.** Anyone can look at a huge chapter and feel discouraged. As you learned in Chapter 1, the trick is to break down your assignment into sections. You may not read and understand 35 pages, but you can read and understand 5 pages. Set that as your goal.

  Divide the work into sections (main headings and subheadings are useful for this) and read one section at a time. You'll get the work done in manageable pieces.

- **Read and respond.** Continue to write questions as you read carefully. You should also take notes. These notes will help you continue to be an active reader. See the section "Note Taking to Get Great Grades" in Chapter 4 for three styles of note taking. You can also use "The Index Card Solution" in Chapter 3.

- **Review.** When you finish reading each section, write a short summary of what you've learned. Summarizing will help you make sense of the information that is now floating around in your brain.

  This is also the time to look back at the questions you wrote as you read. Answer them. If you can't answer them, review the material again. Finally, review all your notes for the reading. Write a summary of the whole assignment.

It's never too late to learn to read. George Washington Carver, who gave the South new industry with his many inventions for the peanut, couldn't read until he was 20.

"There's something called novel time. It takes as long as it takes. "

—Toni Morrison,

writer

Should You Speed Read?

Speed reading is something people argue about. Some people think it's important to read fast. Others say the only thing that matters is how much of your reading you remember. People who believe in speed reading have courses and methods they believe will work. Other people say it is more important to understand what you read, no matter how long it takes. If you can read 1,000 words a minute, but have no idea what you read, what good is it?

There isn't one perfect speed at which to read. Reading at the speed that is right for you will help you remember the beginning of a sentence when you reach the end of the sentence. It will also help you remember the points you read, whether or not you read quickly.

Keep in mind that different kinds of reading require different speeds. If you're deep reading, you'll need more time. If you're skimming, you're looking for a very broad outline or searching for something specific. This won't take as long.

If your reading speed concerns you, try this. Read this section again, beginning with "Speed reading is something people argue about." If it takes you more than 2 or 3 minutes to read, you may need help learning to read faster.

Do you have any of the "Five Reading Habits That Can Slow You Down" listed on the next page? If so, choose one habit and practice changing it over the course of a week. Then choose another habit, until you have learned a new way of reading.

Five Reading Habits That Can Slow You Down

- **Reading aloud to yourself.** Most people speak more slowly than they read. Pronouncing each word as you read can slow you down.

- **Reading each individual word.** Try seeing words as part of phrases. The last sentence, for example, could be broken into "Try seeing words" and "as part of phrases."

- **Using your finger to follow along.** You may be paying more attention to your finger than to the concepts you're reading. You'll also be more likely to concentrate on individual words, not on the way all of the words fit together.

- **Skipping over important words you don't understand.** It may take a little more time to stop and look up a word, but if you don't understand an idea because you don't know an important word, you won't know what you've read.

- **Repeat reading.** Some readers read part of a sentence, then backtrack and read it again. They lose the flow of the author's thinking. If you find yourself doing this, keep going forward. You may find that you do understand the material and that it's just a habit to go backward. Try breaking this habit by previewing your reading.

Should You Highlight?

Your textbook may belong to you. If so, consider doing some of your studying with a highlighter. Underline or *highlight* important phrases and words. Put an arrow ← in the margin to mark a particularly important point. If you don't understand something, write a question mark *?* in the margin.

Use your highlighted notations when you review. Two cautions, though: Don't highlight *instead* of writing your own questions and summaries, and don't repeat the author's work by underlining everything. It's easy to highlight or underline instead of thinking.

If your textbook doesn't belong to you, take notes on a separate sheet of paper on the important phrases, words, and main points you find as you read. Be sure to note only the information that you think is important. Taking too many notes can make reviewing confusing.

Using Your Learning Style as You Read

In Chapter 3, you learned that people have different study styles: listening, seeing, and doing. Try these different ways of remembering what you read. Put your style to work for you.

> **There are many paths up the top of the mountain, but the view is always the same.**
>
> —Chinese proverb

- **Listening.** If you learn best by listening, you're an auditory learner. Tape-record the questions you have as you read, as well as write them. Tape-record your summaries. Then listen to the tape and speak the answers before you write them.

- **Seeing.** If you learn best by looking and picturing what you read, you're a visual learner. Try keeping notes in the idea map style. Draw diagrams and word clusters to help you remember ideas.

- **Doing.** If you learn best by doing, put what you learn into action. When you read a math problem or a science concept, do it. If you're reading a history text, act out the important events.

Here are some suggestions for letting your learning style work for you.

	LISTENING	SEEING	DOING
LANGUAGE ARTS	Write a new scene for a play or story you are reading and perform it for the class.	Watch a videotape of a play, story, or speech you are reading.	Create a model that shows the setting for a story or play.
MATHEMATICS	Tape record a procedure for solving a problem. Then play back your tape and solve the problem step by step.	Draw a picture or diagram of a word problem, then solve it.	Draw a pie graph that shows how you spend your money each week.
SCIENCE	Do an experiment on how fast sound travels through air and water.	Make a word cluster that shows the results of an experiment.	Make a model of the rotations of the planets.
SOCIAL STUDIES	Analyze the music of a culture.	Create a mural that shows an event in history.	Act out a famous debate.

Clued In

Learn More Words!

When you have a large vocabulary, you have a lot of ways to express your ideas. To improve your vocabulary, follow these tips.

- **Keep a set of index cards of words you hear or see and don't know.** Write the word on one side and the definition on the other. When you have a few minutes, review them.

- **Stay on "word alert."** It's easy not to pay attention when you hear or see a new word. Train yourself to stop and write the word down. If you don't have a dictionary handy, make a note to check the definition later.

- **Use context clues.** Look at the words that are near the word you don't know. Often these words will help you figure out the unknown word.

- **Buy a thesaurus.** Tired of using the same old word? Look it up in a thesaurus and find some synonyms. To make sure you're using the new word correctly, look it up in a dictionary.

Did you know?

Literacy rates— the percentage of people in a country who can read—vary greatly in the world. For example, in Belgium 98% of the population can read; in Senegal, 38%; in Saudi Arabia, 65%; in Mexico, 88%; and in the United States, 97.9%.

" I like to hang around words and overhear them whisper to one another. "

—W. H. Auden, poet

CHAPTER CHECKUP

Test yourself on your reading ability. First, choose a reading assignment for one of your classes. After you've finished the assignment, check the techniques in this chapter you've used. Did you

✓ Skim the assignment first to see what to expect?
✓ Read the chapter headings and subheadings?
✓ List questions about the reading as you skimmed?
✓ Divide the assignment into smaller pieces?
✓ Take notes and write questions as you read each section?
✓ Review each section, answering the questions you wrote?
✓ Write a summary of each section?
✓ Write a summary of the entire reading assignment?

Now think about what you learned in this chapter.

1. How can you become an active reader?
2. Which of the five reading habits that slow readers down do you have?
3. What will you do this week to change one of these habits?

[Answers to "Are You Book Smart" on page 32: **1.** e, **2.** a, **3.** b, **4.** d, **5.** c.]

CHAPTER SIX

Becoming Resource Wise

William James, the author of the quotation on this page, must have written a few research papers in his time! When you do research, the possibilities can seem endless. There are books, magazine articles, almanacs, encyclopedias, people, and even the Internet to check. Where do you start? How can you make sense of the many possibilities?

Help is on the way. This chapter will help you begin, conduct, and finish your research. You'll learn how to find printed materials. The Reference section at the end of this book also lists Internet sites that you can use for your research. In addition, you'll learn

- How to tell if a book will give you the information you need.
- How to use the parts of a book.
- How to find what you need in a library.
- How to choose from the resources available.
- How to keep track of the information you find.
- How to make the Internet work for you.

Is It the Right Book?

You can save time in the library if you can judge whether a book has the information you need. Here are some clues.

- **Look at the table of contents.** If you're looking for a general reference book on a topic, the table of contents should show you the main ideas in the book.

- **Check the index.** If you're looking for something specific, the index will tell you if the book has information on your topic and where the information is located.

- **Look up similar words or topics in the index.** Sometimes indexes don't think the way you do. For example, instead of a specific topic, look up the name of a person who has been involved with the topic.

- **Check the pages listed in the index.** The book may have just what you need—or it may not.

> **"The art of being wise is the art of knowing what to overlook."**
> —William James,
> philosopher

The Parts of a Book

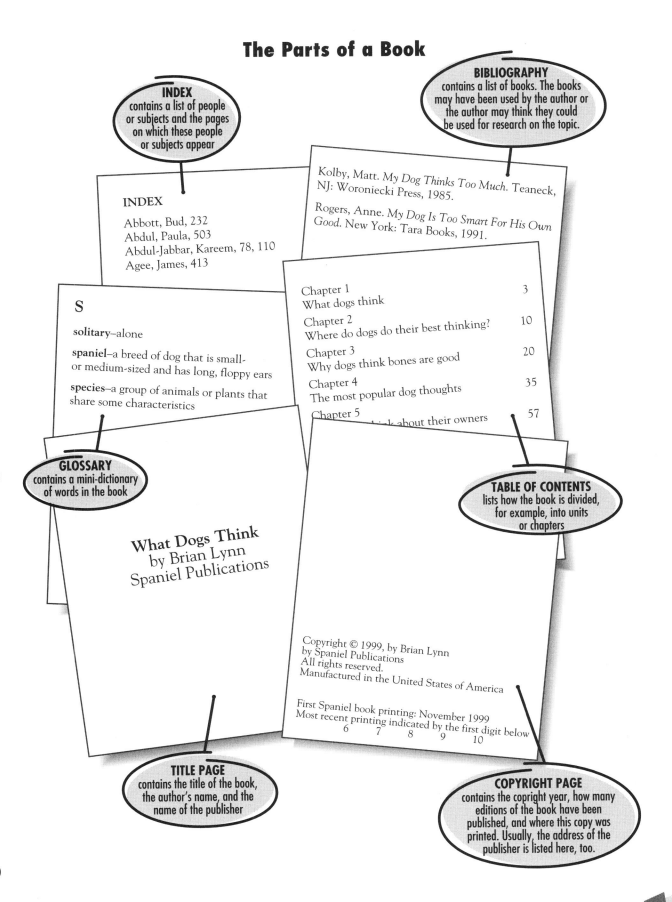

INDEX
contains a list of people or subjects and the pages on which these people or subjects appear

BIBLIOGRAPHY
contains a list of books. The books may have been used by the author or the author may think they could be used for research on the topic.

INDEX

Abbott, Bud, 232
Abdul, Paula, 503
Abdul-Jabbar, Kareem, 78, 110
Agee, James, 413

Kolby, Matt. *My Dog Thinks Too Much.* Teaneck, NJ: Woroniecki Press, 1985.

Rogers, Anne. *My Dog Is Too Smart For His Own Good.* New York: Tara Books, 1991.

S

solitary–alone

spaniel–a breed of dog that is small- or medium-sized and has long, floppy ears

species–a group of animals or plants that share some characteristics

GLOSSARY
contains a mini-dictionary of words in the book

TABLE OF CONTENTS
lists how the book is divided, for example, into units or chapters

What Dogs Think
by Brian Lynn
Spaniel Publications

Copyright © 1999, by Brian Lynn
by Spaniel Publications
All rights reserved.
Manufactured in the United States of America

First Spaniel book printing: November 1999
Most recent printing indicated by the first digit below
6   7   8   9   10

TITLE PAGE
contains the title of the book, the author's name, and the name of the publisher

COPYRIGHT PAGE
contains the copright year, how many editions of the book have been published, and where this copy was printed. Usually, the address of the publisher is listed here, too.

Where Can You Find It?

Do you know the best place to find these things?

1. Population of Zaire
2. Origin of the word *insect*
3. Synonym for *delicious*
4. Birthdate of Prince Charles of Great Britain
5. Recent articles on space exploration
6. History of Paris
7. Tallest man in the world
8. Information on the commercial airplane crashes in 1996

a. encyclopedia
b. *Guinness Book of Records*
c. unabridged dictionary
d. *Facts on File*
e. *World Almanac*
f. thesaurus
g. *Current Biography*
h. *Reader's Guide to Periodical Literature*

(Answers are on page 50.)

Finding What You Need in the Library

There are differences between libraries, but most have many things in common. Most libraries have sections with books that can be checked out and reference sections, in which the materials can be used only in the library. The reference section has books such as encyclopedias and almanacs that many people look at during a day. Your library, however, may have old copies of these books to check out. Many libraries put the previous year's almanac in the regular collection. Some information, like the capital cities of countries, usually doesn't change (but check!).

How Libraries Are Organized

Most libraries arrange books in one of two ways. They use either the Dewey Decimal System or the Library of Congress System. Most use the Dewey Decimal System. This system was created by super-librarian Melvil Dewey in 1876.

Here's a brief rundown of how the Dewey system works. First, Dewey divided all human knowledge into 10 categories.

000–099	General Works
100–199	Philosophy
200–299	Religion

> **What is more important in a library than anything else—than everything else—is the fact that it exists.**
>
> — Archibald MacLeish, poet

300–399	Social Sciences
400–499	Language
500–599	Science
600–699	Applied Science
700–799	Fine Arts
800–899	Literature
900–999	History

Within these categories are subcategories. For example, the history category also contains biography, geography, and travel books. The numbers also indicate subcategories. For example, the number 973 is applied to books about the history of African Americans in the United States.

The Library of Congress system uses letters as well as numbers. It has 21 categories in which to classify books. Larger libraries often use this system because it offers a variety of ways to group books.

Finding the Books You Need

Clued In

- **Card catalogs.** Many school libraries are not yet computerized. If your school isn't computerized, the card catalog is your search tool there. You can look up information by title, subject, or author. Copy the title, the author, and the *entire* call number. Without the entire number, you may not be able to find the book you want.

- **Electronic catalogs.** Almost all local, city, and college libraries today use electronic card catalogs. Systems differ, but they usually are user friendly. Computer catalogs walk you through your search. You can usually search by subject, author, or title. Although you may have to write down the information you need, you might be able to print a copy of your search list. That will save you time and energy—and help you make sure you have all of the information you need.

- **Library tours.** With the wide range of information now available in most local libraries, a tour is helpful. For example, you can learn how to find a book faster by bypassing many of the search screens. You'll also find out how to get interlibrary loans, which allow you to borrow books from other libraries.

- **Look around.** Once you go to the shelves to find a book, you may want to look at the books near the one you've chosen.

These books may not have come up on screen because they have a slightly different subject, but they may have other information you can use.

- **Can't find a book on the shelf?** First, check the area near where the book should be. It may have been misshelved. Next, check the call number you've written. If the book is marked REF, it's in the reference section, not on the regular shelves.

  If it's not in the reference section and your library has an electronic system, check the computer. The screen will show if the book is checked out. If so, you may need to put the book on hold, which means the library will call you when it's returned. Also ask the librarian to check if the book has been returned but not yet reshelved.

Using People Resources in a Library

Many libraries have research librarians whose job is to help people find things. These people can point you in new directions. They can show you how to use the computers to access another world of information. They can arrange for interlibrary loans. Use these librarians. They're the most neglected resource in the library. They can save you time—and frustration.

A Guide to Often-Used Resource Books

Remember the quiz on page 42 about what to find and where to find it? Here's a rundown of what those books contain and when to use them.

Encyclopedias

You probably know about these many-volume sets. Encyclopedias contain articles that give an overview of many subjects. There are also encyclopedias that have only one volume. These can help you find a general fact.

At the end of the entries in most multi-volume encyclopedias, there are bibliographic references. These are lists of books and sources for the information in the entry. They can help you find more detailed information. Encyclopedias also publish yearly additions, called *yearbooks*. Look in these if you're looking for an event in a year that has a yearbook.

In addition to general encyclopedias, there are specialized encyclopedias. These may focus on science, nature, medicine, geography, or other subjects.

Did you know

Libraries date back to 3000 B.C., when the Sumerians set up central locations for clay tablets with business and legal information. The largest library of the ancient world was built by the Greeks in Alexandria, Egypt, in 300 B.C. This library had 700,000 papyrus and linen rolls. It even had an area for translating and copying these texts.

Almanacs

Almanacs are great places to find statistics. For example, look in an almanac (make sure it's the current year) for information on populations, heads of state, and the name of last year's Super Bowl champion. In addition, almanacs have facts about countries around the world, some maps, and reference information such as a listing of all the chemical elements that have been discovered. An almanac is one book that may be worth buying every year for your home library.

Dictionaries

Dictionaries have information well beyond the meanings of words. In the beginning of each entry, you can find how to pronounce words. (At the bottom of each page in most dictionaries, a key shows you how to use the pronunciation symbols.)

Following the pronunciation is information on the word's history and which language the word comes from. Finally, you'll see the word's definition. The first listed definition is the way the word is most commonly used. Here is an example.

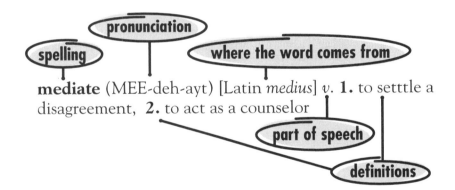

mediate (MEE-deh-ayt) [Latin *medius*] *v.* **1.** to setttle a disagreement, **2.** to act as a counselor

Thesaurus

A thesaurus can help you find the right word. Many word processing programs now contain a thesaurus. You click on a word, click on the thesaurus key, and a list of synonyms appears. Thesauruses such as *Roget's* are also available in book form, of course.

Be careful of the words you choose in a thesaurus. A thesaurus lists *synonyms*, not substitutes, for the word you're looking for. Check the word's meaning in a dictionary to be sure it means *exactly* what you want to say. Don't overlook the thesaurus for finding antonyms. At the end of many entries are words that mean the opposite of the word you looked up. These can be handy, too.

Facts on File

These books are the perfect resource if you're looking for news on a current event. They contain short accounts of news articles and are compiled yearly. They have indexes you can use to pinpoint topics. If you find the account, but don't have enough information, write down all the information about the article. If it is from a major national newspaper such as *The New York Times*, a librarian can probably help you find the original article.

Magazine Guides

The magazine guide you may know is the *Reader's Guide to Periodical Literature*. This guide is printed several times a year. It lists all the magazine articles in major magazines by subject. You can locate articles you want to see, then find out if your library has the magazines in which they were published. Your librarian might also be able to get a copy of the magazine from another library. Here is a sample entry from the *Reader's Guide to Periodical Literature*.

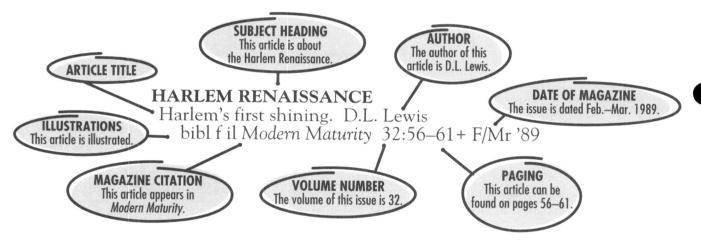

Many libraries now have computerized magazine searches such as the Magazine Index. Your librarian can show you how to use them. Your library may also have a user-friendly system that walks you through the steps to finding the articles you need. One advantage to many of these computer-based searches is that they allow you to print summaries or articles while you are working on the computer.

Current Biography

Current Biography is a magazine that publishes profiles of people in the news. It was first published in 1940. *Current Biography* has an index to help you find people who have been profiled. For people who were well-known before 1940, you'll have to check with other sources.

Guinness Book of Records

The *Guinness Book of Records* began in England when two men made a bet and couldn't find the information they needed to find out who was right. Today, the book contains some strange information, such as the size of the world's largest pizza.

It can be useful for other information, though. For example, it is the authority on sports records, natural disasters, and modern wonders, such as the world's tallest building. You can use it to add spice to a report on hurricanes or to find the name of the world's largest mammal.

Look Beyond Books

Many libraries have an amazing number of resources that aren't books.

- **Microfilm and microfiche.** Many magazines and newspapers are photographed and transferred to small pieces of film so that they're easier to store and use. Microfilm is on reels, and microfiche is on sheets or cards. To read either, you need a machine that enlarges what you see. A librarian can show you how to do this. It's easy to learn, but don't try it on your own. You may damage the materials. One advantage to these materials is that often you can slip in a coin and make a copy of the page you're reading.

- **AV materials.** These are audio tapes, videotapes, CD-ROMs, laser discs, and compact discs. Don't overlook these materials. They can provide different information than books. Listening to a speech, for example, can tell you about the person's speaking style, the audience's response, and what it was like to be there. These sources can also be useful for a presentation.

- **Maps, photographs, and artwork.** Libraries also include collections of maps and art. You may be able to check these out or copy them to add interest to a report.

Keeping Track of Resources

If you begin a project without a plan for keeping track of what you're doing, you're doomed. You'll be frustrated by not being able to find books you need and forgetting where you've already looked. To avoid this, you'll need to organize your research.

Most people use index cards to keep track of research, although some take notes in notebooks. Whichever way you choose, you need to do this.

1. Write down each book you use or think you might use. Write the title, the author, the call number, and the library where you found the book. Many teachers also require that you write the information you need for footnotes or endnotes and a bibliography: the year the book was published, who published it, and where it was published. (There's more on when and how to use this information in Chapter 9, "Writing a Research Paper.")

2. Keep a list of the books you are using, or think you might use, in one place. That's why many people use index cards— they put one book or resource on each card and keep the cards together.

3. When you find information you need, write it on another card. At the top of the card, write the title of the book and the pages you used. Write only one fact or information about only one subject area on each card. This will allow you to organize your research easily.

Clued In

Mastering the Internet

Millions of computers and people throughout the world are linked through the Internet. How can the "Net" help you? If you're computer literate, you know you can use it to find software or friends, send mail, and talk to people in other

Did you know?

The record for an overdue library book was set in England. In 1667, Colonel Robert Walpole took out a book from the Sidney Sussex College Library. It was returned 288 years later. There was no fine.

countries. You can find government documents and recipes for apple pie, and you can tap into libraries around the world.

The Net can also help you research a topic for a paper. How do you get onto the Internet?

- First, you need access to a computer with a modem. That might be a computer at school or at home. If you have a modem at home, you might find that the easiest way to get onto the Internet is through an on-line service. These services include America Online, CompuServe, Prodigy, and a number of others. Each has step-by-step instructions for how to move around the Net. Your town library might also have a computer that you can use to search the Net.

- Using the Net is similar to using the computer search for books at the library. You type in a subject and the screen shows you possible sources of information. You click on one of these, and the computer connects you to that site on the Net. If that site does not have the information you need, you simply click on the next site.

- It can take a little while to figure out how to ask for specific information in a search, so keep trying. You may find that it's worthwhile to take a class that can help you learn the ins and outs of the Net. An experienced computer user can help you choose words and sites that have the information you need.

How much did you learn about using resources? Test yourself.

Imagine that you are assigned a research project. You may choose one of the following topics:

✓ the religious beliefs of the Plains Indians

✓ the music of Latin America

✓ the endangered wildlife of Africa

List as many kinds of resources as you can that might help you do your research.

If you found 5 or more sources, congratulations. You know your way around the library. If you listed 3 to 4 sources, you could use more work with this chapter. If you only listed 1 or 2 sources, ask your librarian for some additional help.

Your resource skills will be useful in your life outside of school. For example, you'll be able to buy a car or plan a vacation wisely. Books and magazines can advise you on making good choices.

Now think about what you learned in this chapter.

1. What tips could you give another student for finding information?

2. List at least three often-used resource books.

3. Why is the Internet a good research tool?

(Answers to "Where Can You Find It?" on page 42: **1.** e, **2.** c, **3.** f, **4.** g, **5.** h, **6.** a, **7.** b, **8.** d)

CHAPTER SEVEN

The Art of Taking Tests

Whole books have been written about how to take tests. There may be no subject that fills students with more anxiety. If you follow the suggestions in this chapter, you may never fear tests again. You will learn

- How to study for tests.

- How and why to avoid cramming.

- How to control test anxiety.

- How to do well on different kinds of tests, from essay to multiple choice.

- How to handle standardized tests.

- How to use tests to review for final exams.

How Do You Get Ready for a Test?

How many of these things do you do before you take a test?

- Realize you've forgotten last week's lessons

- Put off studying and cram the night before

- Just look through your notes

- Memorize all of your notes

- Don't really know when the test is

- Get so anxious you can't concentrate

- Prepare for all tests the same way

- Get so overwhelmed that you give up studying

If any of these statements describes you, you need a test-taking tune-up. Read on.

Ace That Test!

Put these strategies to work for you.

- **Review all along.** The best part of learning how to study is that you'll be almost ready for any test, whether it's a quiz or a final. If you follow the tips in Chapter 3 for studying, you're already reviewing both after every study session and weekly. By the time a test comes around, you'll know the information.

—Wynton Marsalis, musician

> **"You won't get anywhere without sweat."**

- **Test yourself.** You can create a test that's similar to the one your teacher will give you. Use your notes and book to help you. Create questions that test main ideas and details. Create other questions that help you connect the facts you've learned. Then create questions that show you can apply what you've learned to a new situation.

- **Use your study group.** One of the best times to use a study group is when you're studying for tests. You might have each group member write questions about a different section of the material. You might also have everyone write a test. Then have people take turns at answering each other's tests, or assemble all of the questions and create a master test that you all take.

- **Don't review everything.** You can spend hours studying for a test and still not know what you need to know. As you begin your final review, start with the main ideas. From there, study the details that support the main ideas. Also study anything your teacher has said will be on the test. Don't get bogged down in tiny details.

- **Memorize the formulas**. Make sure you know by heart anything you need to memorize to do well. All of this information should be on cards you've already studied. (See Chapter 3 to review the "The Index Card Solution.") Then just look over your cards to double-check that you know the material that you've studied.

Got It?

Before you walk into a test, be prepared. Whatever you're going to need, bring it. Just in case, check this list the night before your test. See if anything you need is on it. If something is on the list, set it aside the night before. This way, you will only have to think about taking the test the next morning.

✓ pencils   ✓ pens

✓ eraser   ✓ paper

✓ watch   ✓ calculator

✓ ruler   ✓ protractor

✓ compass

A Few Words About Cramming . . .

Don't do it. Why not? First, you won't be able to remember information that you've dumped into your head the night before. Second, if you stay up late cramming, you'll be in poor shape to take a test. Third, whatever you do manage to cram into your head will be gone long before the next test.

Are You Afraid of Tests?

Are you anxious before a test? You're not alone. It's easy to get so nervous that you can't even tell if a test is a heart-stopper or a breeze.

- Do you walk into a test feeling sure you won't do well?

- Do you rarely feel that you're prepared for a test?

- Do you walk into tests short of breath or with sweaty palms?

- Do you panic when you don't know an answer?

- Do you feel that you never study enough, no matter how well-prepared you are?

- Do you forget things you know when you walk into a test?

If you said yes to any of the questions above, you're a candidate for "Taming Test Fears" below.

Taming Test Fears

If you can develop test anxiety, you can beat it. Here's how.

- Make sure you're prepared. Create a sample test and answer all of the questions to take the edge off that terror.

- Don't walk in and immediately start answering questions. Look at the entire test first. Figure out which will be the easy parts and which will be the hard parts. Then decide how much time you'll need for each one.

- Next, make your own "crib sheet." If there are formulas or central facts you need to know to do well, write them on the back of the test. It will be comforting to know they're there.

- Do an easy part first. It will boost your confidence.

- Take a deep breath. If you find yourself panicking, sit back. Close your eyes for three seconds. Take a deep breath. Let it out slowly. Do it again. Now open your eyes. You'll feel calmer.

- Don't pay attention to anyone else. The best students don't necessarily finish first. Listening to the groans of people around you won't help you, either. Tune them out.

- Keep a positive attitude. If you tell yourself you'll do well, you probably will. If you tell yourself you won't do well, you probably won't.

General Rules for Success on Any Test

Whether it's a closed-book or an open-book test, an essay, or a true/false test, some rules about taking tests apply every time.

> **Strive to be the best you can be and remember that when you try your best, you can't ask any more from yourself and people can't ask any more from you.**
>
> —Michael Chang, athlete

- **Be there on time.** Make an extra effort to get to the classroom before the test starts. That way, you can start getting ready to take the test. More importantly, you won't be coming in late and starting with a disadvantage.

- **Take a look at the entire test.** This is similar to the advice for reading an assignment. If you know what's coming, you can design your time better. You can also get a good sense for what the teacher wants you to know.

- **Make a plan.** Schedule your time by checking how many points will be assigned to each section. For example, if you know the essay questions count for two-thirds of the points in the test, spend about two-thirds of your time there. Stick closely to your schedule. Then, if you have time at the end of the test, you can go back to a section that you didn't quite finish. This way, you won't run out of time before you run out of questions.

- **Read the directions.** Misunderstanding directions is the biggest reason for disappointing test results. Before you begin a part of the test, reread the directions to make sure you've got them right.

- **Neatness counts.** Think about how you respond to a messy paper and how you respond to a neat one. Then do your best to keep it neat.

- **Make sure you've answered all the questions.** If you have time after you've finished, make sure you did everything you were supposed to do. Check to make sure you didn't miss a question.

Test Code Words and What They Mean

Words in test directions mean specific things. Here's a list.

Word	Description
Define or summarize	Write a brief answer stating the most important points listed.
Compare	Tell how two things are alike.
Contrast	Tell how two things are different.
Analyze	Go deeper and explain how things are related.
Illustrate	Give examples.
Discuss	Write about all the angles of a topic.
List	Do exactly that— no details.
Explain	Give the reasons for something.
Describe	Give the main idea and the details.

Tips for Taking Objective Tests

Objective tests are tests that usually have one right answer. They often include true/false, fill in the blanks, and multiple-choice questions. You can improve your scores on objective tests by using these tips.

General Tips

- Underline or circle the important words in the directions. They may ask you to pick the *wrong* answer instead of the right one.

- Know if there is a penalty for guessing. If there isn't, answer every question. If there is a penalty for guessing, you may be better off skipping a question.

- Be sneaky. Look for grammar. If a choice doesn't fit grammatically, it probably isn't the right answer. For example, if a question asks for the cause<u>s</u> of the Civil War, the answer must have more than one cause.

- Should you change your first answer? Maybe. If you've remembered information that will help you make a better choice, use it. If you've misread a question, change your answer. If you feel strongly about an answer, chances are it's right.

- Neatness counts. If an "F" looks like a "T," it will be marked wrong.

True/False Tips

- If you see *never* and *always* on a true/false test, be careful. There's often an exception to these absolute words that makes the correct answer "false."

- If you see *sometimes* and *often* in a question, look at the answers closely. As mentioned in the previous tip, there are few absolutes. Answers to these questions are often "true."

- If a true/false question is long and involved, its answer is more likely to be "false." Why? Every part of the statement must be correct for the answer to be "true."

Multiple-Choice Tips

- Instead of looking at the answers and picking one, answer the question yourself and see if your answer matches one of the choices.

"It's Been a Hard Day's Night."
—John Lennon and Paul McCartney, songwriters

- If you can eliminate one or more answers, guess.

- Remember, though, there's no such thing as a magic formula. Just because you haven't marked "B" for a while, it's not necessarily time for one now.

- If you see the right answer and mark "C" without reading on, you may not realize that "D" is correct, too. In this case, the correct answer may be "E: both C and D."

- One way to know if "all of the above" is true on a multiple-choice test is to see if you can find more than one answer that is true. If it is, "all of the above" must be the answer.

Clued In

Tips for Taking Subjective Tests

Subjective tests are also called essay tests. They're called *subjective* because the questions can be answered in many different ways. Don't let them scare you. Subjective tests give you a chance to show what you know. Use these tips to improve your scores on subjective tests.

- Read the directions carefully. Underline the important words in the directions as a reminder. Do exactly what the question asks you to do.

- Make sure you know what the code words mean. (See "Test Code Words and What They Mean" on page 55.)

- Outline your answer. It can be a formal Roman-numeral outline or an informal cluster drawing. An outline can help you make sure that you state all of your arguments and that you present them in a logical order.

- Write an opening statement that states your main idea. The next paragraphs should have examples and facts that back up your main idea. The final paragraph should be a conclusion that restates your main idea.

- You can support your main idea with facts, which are details that can be proven; examples, which show evidence for your main idea; and reasons, which tell how or why something happened.

- Think about the style of answer your teacher prefers. If he or she favors a straightforward style, use that. On the other hand, if your teacher rewards emotional appeals or well-crafted language, use these.

- Watch the time. If you find yourself falling behind schedule, pay less attention to style and more to making sure you include your important points.

The first known written school exams were given in 1817 in England. The students had to know English, Latin, Greek, history, geography, and religion. The tests lasted 1½ to 2 hours and were given before breakfast. The students had no idea which of the subjects they would be tested on.

I don't believe in inspiration. I believe in hard work.

—Isabel Allende,

writer

- Keep it neat. You don't want your teacher to mistake one word for another. Also, a neat paper looks like you've approached the test seriously and that you've done your homework.

- Check your work to make sure that it makes sense and that it follows from point to point.

- Proofread your work. Correct grammar and spelling errors.

The Four Types of Essay Tests

Essays fall into four basic categories. If you know what type of question your teacher is asking, you'll have a better chance of answering it correctly.

1. **Persuasive essay.** Persuasive essay questions often will ask you to give your opinion or convince a reader about something. Answer these questions by stating your opinion and backing up that opinion with reasons and examples. Persuasive essays should also answer issues that might be raised by someone who has a different opinion.

2. **Descriptive essay.** Descriptive essay questions often will ask you to describe or picture something. These essays succeed when the description paints a clear picture for the reader. Often, using details that relate to the five senses (sight, hearing, smell, taste, and touch) can work well.

3. **Expository essay.** Many essay tests ask you for expository essays. These essays tell how something works or how something is done. Often, the directions ask you to compare and contrast two or more ideas or people or to explain your solution to a problem. These essays require logic and details that back up your points.

4. **Narrative essay.** Narrative essays ask for stories from your experience or stories that you create. A narrative essay may also ask you to describe how and why you made a difficult decision. You can best answer these questions by focusing on one good example and then telling the story in a way that shows how this story makes your point.

Standardized Test Do's and Don'ts

There are a few differences between tests your teacher creates and standardized tests, such as PSATs, SATs, and IOWAs. Your teacher's tests are designed to find out what you've learned in his or her class. Standardized tests are designed to find out what you've learned throughout your school career. To do well on standardized tests, review the tips for taking tests that are listed throughout this chapter. Then read these guidelines to help you prepare further for standardized tests.

✓ Do

1. Take any sample tests that your school has available. They can help you become familiar with the kinds of questions to expect.

2. Make sure you're answering the right question. When you take standardized tests that have rows of numbers and answers, it's easy to miss a line. Missing a line means every answer will be wrong.

3. Start at the beginning. Many standardized tests go from easier to harder questions.

4. Be sure to complete the parts that take the least time and that you know best. Objective questions are often worth the same amount of points.

5. Get comfortable. Wear clothing in layers you can put on or take off. If you're allowed to, bring something to eat and drink during breaks. Food can give you extra energy. Also, stretch during breaks. Stretching can keep your brain active. Need an extra break to clear your head? Ask to go to the bathroom and splash some cold water on your face.

✗ Don't

1. Assume that because you can't study for a standardized test, you can't prepare for it.

2. Begin the test without reviewing it. Instead, look for the number of points given for each section, and divide your time so that you don't leave out a section.

3. Answer questions you don't have a clue about. Most standardized tests take points off for wrong answers. (Find out if that's true for the tests you will take.) Instead, put a small mark by the question so you can find it again. Another question may jog your memory, or the answer may suddenly occur to you.

4. Turn your test in if you finish early. Instead, review your answers.

Think You're Done With That Test?

Even if you think you never want to see it again, keep that test after your teacher gives it back to you. While the test is still fresh in your mind, fill in the correct answers. Tests can help you review material for final exams.

Now look at where you tend to make errors and why. Did you misread the directions? Did you miss questions about a specific area of the course? Did you lose points for sloppiness? Did you have trouble with certain kinds of questions? Use your returned test as a tool. Figure out where you need help, whether it's in taking tests or in subject matter. Then make a plan for learning what you need to improve.

CHAPTER CHECKUP

Check your test-taking skills by taking this test.

The questions in sections 1 and 2 are worth 5 points each. Section 3 is worth 50 points. You have 20 minutes.

Section 1

Decide whether each statement is true or false.

1. You should always study everything from the course when you study for a test.

2. Making up tests can help you study.

3. When you are told to begin a test, immediately begin answering the questions in order.

4. Teachers know you're under pressure, so don't bother to be neat. It's more important to get the information down than to care about how you write it.

5. If a true/false question is long and involved, it's always false.

Section 2

Choose the letter that best completes each sentence.

1. All of the following are good techniques for studying for a test *except*
   a. memorizing formulas you need.
   b. reviewing everything from the course.
   c. using your study group to review course work.
   d. making up a test and then taking it.
   e. reviewing every day.

2. You can beat test anxiety by doing all of the following *except*
   a. doing the hardest part of the test first to give you confidence.
   b. taking a deep breath and closing your eyes.
   c. looking at the entire test before you start.
   d. writing down the formulas and facts you need on the back of the test.
   e. ignoring what others in the class are doing.

3. All of the following tips can help you succeed in any test *except*

   a. making a plan for how you will complete the test.

   b. turning in your test as soon as you finish answering the last question.

   c. reading the directions, then rereading them if you have time.

   d. scheduling your time so that you spend more time on questions that are worth more points.

   e. arriving on time.

4. You can improve your scores on objective tests by doing all of the following *except*

   a. double-checking the directions.

   b. spending an equal amount of time on every question.

   c. writing neatly.

   d. knowing if there is a penalty for guessing.

   e. guessing an answer if you can eliminate one or more choices.

5. You can improve your scores on subjective tests by doing all of the following *except*

   a. considering what kind of writing your teacher likes.

   b. making an outline before you start.

   c. ignoring the time.

   d. understanding the code words in the questions.

   e. making sure your essay has a beginning, a middle, and an end.

Section 3

Write a short essay about one of the following questions.

   1. Compare the best ways to take objective and subjective tests.

   2. Summarize the best way to study for a test.

   3. Describe the best ways to handle test anxiety.

Now think about what you learned in this chapter.

   1. What strategies do you use when you study for a test?

   2. How do you beat test anxiety?

CHAPTER EIGHT

The Art of Writing

Everyone writes. It may be a grocery list, a memo to a boss, or a best-seller, but everyone does it. It's wise, then, to learn to write easily, and clearly. In this chapter, you'll learn

- The different kinds of writing.

- How different audiences affect your writing style.

- Why you should write on a computer if you have one.

- How to cure writer's block.

- How to brainstorm writing ideas.

- How to turn your notes into a finished paper.

Why You Write

Whole books have been written about the different kinds of writing. Here's a quick overview of what you need to know.

- **Writing to inform or explain.** When you write to inform or explain, you should have a main point and details that back up that main point. At the end of the piece, your reader should understand your ideas and why you think as you do. *Things to check:* The main idea is clear. I've backed it up with evidence. My ideas flow smoothly into one another.

- **Writing to describe.** When you write to describe, you tell about a person, a place, or a thing. Examples of descriptive writing might include a profile of your grandmother or a piece that tells about a place you visited. *Things to check:* My reader can picture my subject exactly. I used words that appeal to the five senses.

- **Writing a narrative.** A narrative tells a story. This story can be either fictional or real. Both your autobiography and a story about a person landing on Saturn can be written as narratives. *Things to check:* I've included all of the details a reader needs to follow my story.

- **Writing to persuade.** You write to persuade when you try to convince someone about an opinion you have. You can persuade someone by stating your opinion clearly and choosing facts and examples that support it. Letters to the editor are examples of persuasive writing. *Things to check:* I've presented evidence to support my point of view.

Clued In

Who Is Your Audience?

Before you start to write, think about how you can best reach your audience. For example, you might describe your favorite song quite differently to a friend and to a parent. When you think about your audience, think about the information that people need and how they will best understand it. Here are some things to ask yourself before you write.

- How much does my audience know about the subject?
  If you're writing a letter to the editor of the school paper about the school dress code, you need to include less background. If you're writing a letter on the same topic to your town's newspaper, you need more background. If you're in doubt, assume you need to add background. It's better to have extra details than to lose your audience. Explain the technical terms and background that are necessary to understanding what you write.

- Does my audience agree with me?
  You would write one speech for a group of students that agree with you that the dress code must go. You'd write another speech for a group of parents that have fought to get the dress code in place. If you know that your audience needs convincing, you might say, "Although many people believe that a dress code is necessary, there are good reasons to consider revising or getting rid of it."

- Would my audience prefer formal or informal writing?
  Your teacher might not like slang, but your friends might think you're not cool if you don't use it. Most of your papers for school will have a formal style. An informal style is appropriate for letters to friends.

" There is no rule on how to write. Sometimes it comes easily and perfectly; sometimes it's like drilling rock and then blasting out with charges. "
—Ernest Hemingway,
writer

Ways You Write

Writing can take many forms, from a poem to a science report. Each form of writing has its own features. You may prefer one form of writing over another. For example, if you like to express your point of view, you may enjoy writing letters to the editor. On the other hand, if you like to create stories, you may enjoy writing fiction. If you do prefer one form of writing, ask your teacher if he or she will accept a letter to the editor or a short story instead of a straight report for an assignment. Your teacher may think that your request is a creative way to approach an assignment, and you may find it more fun to do.

Should You Use a Computer?

You may not own a computer, but you may have access to one. Your school may have a computer. Your local library may have one that you can use. Your teacher may be able to tell you where you can have access to a computer.

If you can find a computer, it probably makes sense to use one. Why?

- Your work will look better. As you've read in earlier chapters in this book, neatness counts. A computer can help you produce neatly typed work. You can also center a title and number pages for a polished look.

- You can easily make additions, deletions, and changes. If you make a typing error, or you want to move a paragraph, change is as easy as a keystroke.

- You can check your spelling. A spelling tool will point out words you misspelled, even ones that you thought you had spelled correctly. Be careful, though. The computer can't tell the difference between *their* and *there*. Both are words, so both will pass the spell checker, even if you've used the wrong word.

- You can check your grammar. Almost all word processing programs now have grammar-checking programs. These programs can tell you when a sentence isn't complete, when you use the same word too often, and so on. Be careful with this tool, though. Some grammar checkers misunderstand the point you're trying to make.

- You can draw graphs, tables, and other attractive graphics with the computer.

- You will probably use computers in school, in college, or on the job. If you learn your way around computers now, they'll be a snap when you have to use them later.

Some people just love to write. Lewis Carroll, who wrote *Alice's Adventures in Wonderland*, wrote 98,721 letters during the last 40 years of his life.

Chipping Off the Writer's Block

Almost everyone has experienced that terrible moment when it seems as if there is *nothing* to write. Your mind may feel as blank as the paper or computer screen in front of you. Writer John McPhee used to get up in the morning and tie himself to his chair with the tie of his bathrobe, just to force himself to sit and write. And you thought you had trouble!

> **"The artist must say it without saying it."**
> —Duke Ellington, musician

Sometimes just knowing that you're not alone is helpful in beating writer's block. If you still need help, try these hints.

- **Free associate.** Just sit down and write whatever comes to mind. At least you'll get started, and something you write may help you think. It's less discouraging to continue when you've at least started your work.

- **Type a paragraph from an author whose work you admire.** Sometimes just the act of putting well-written words on paper can inspire you. Make sure, though, that you footnote this paragraph if you use it in your work.

- **Try a different form of writing.** For example, write the information in the form of a poem instead of as a report.

- **Call a friend and discuss your ideas.** Sometimes you can get unstuck by talking with someone.

- **Write in the style of an author whose work you like.**

- **Try another form of expression.** Play a musical instrument. Use some modeling clay and make a sculpture of your subject.

- **Get out of your rut.** Do some heavy exercise. Start another assignment. Come back to your writing when you're refreshed.

- **Don't panic when you're stuck.** Move on to another part of your writing and come back to the problem part later. There's no rule that you have to write in order.

- **Don't be too hard on yourself.** What you write doesn't have to be perfect. It just has to say what you want to say.

Make Any Writing Better

There are a few general rules for writing. Your writing should make sense. It should have a point. It should flow from one point to the next. It should be free of spelling, grammar, and punctuation errors. Follow these steps when you're doing any kind of writing. They will improve the quality of your work.

1. **Be sure you understand what the teacher wants.** Is it a paragraph? a list? a 10-page paper? Whatever the assignment is, plan to deliver it.

2. **Brainstorm a list of ideas.** This list should have everything that comes to mind, from the important to the silly.

3. **Use the best of your brainstormed ideas.** What topic will you choose? What points will you make? How will you support your points? Begin to focus on your topic by circling or underlining the ideas you will use.

4. **Turn your notes into a plan.** You can make an outline or an idea map. You can also choose another way to organize your thinking. When you make your plan, be sure that your ideas flow from one to another. Also be sure that you have details or examples to support your main points. (Review Chapter 4 for tips on making and using outlines and idea maps.)

5. **Write a first draft.** Don't worry about spelling and grammar. Instead, just put your ideas on paper. Don't worry if words are crossed out and little arrows lead to sentences on the sides of the pages. A first draft is just for you.

6. **Rewrite your paper.** Make sure your main point is clear and that it is supported with evidence or details. Make sure you have an introduction and a conclusion and that your ideas flow. Check spelling, grammar, and punctuation.

7. **Neatness counts.** If your paper is messy, recopy it.

"...with words I have the power to make people listen, to make them think in a new way, to make them cry, to make them laugh."

—Sandra Cisneros, writer

CHAPTER CHECKUP

Use this writing checklist after you've written the second draft of an essay you've been assigned. Make sure you've covered all of the bases.

Topic
✓ Is the topic of your writing focused (not too narrow or too broad)?
✓ Is it what your teacher assigned?

Purpose and Audience
✓ What is your purpose for writing?
✓ Will the writing appeal to your audience?

Organization
✓ Does your writing have an introduction that states the topic?
✓ Do the details or examples support this topic?
✓ Are your facts correct?
✓ Do your ideas flow from one to the next?
✓ Does your writing have an ending that restates your topic?

Words
✓ Are you sure you used the right word?
✓ Are all the words spelled correctly?

Grammar
✓ Is the meaning of each sentence clear?
✓ Do the subjects and verbs agree?

Punctuation
✓ Does each sentence begin with a capital letter and end with a period, exclamation mark, or question mark?

Style
✓ Is your writing clear and easy to understand?
✓ Do you vary the way your sentences begin and end?
✓ Do you have a title page?

Now think about what you learned in this chapter.
1. Why is your audience so important to your writing?
2. List three things you can do to improve your writing.

CHAPTER NINE

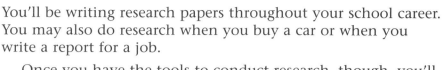

Writing a Research Paper

You'll be writing research papers throughout your school career. You may also do research when you buy a car or when you write a report for a job.

Once you have the tools to conduct research, though, you'll approach these assignments with confidence. In this chapter, you'll learn how to

- Choose a topic.

- Organize your research.

- Conduct an interview.

- Take notes that will make writing your paper a breeze.

- Organize your research.

- Write a research paper.

- Construct footnotes and bibliographies.

- Create a professional-looking finished paper.

Research Readiness

Research papers strike fear into the hearts of some students. If you choose the right topic, however, writing a research paper can be a breeze.

Most teachers give you some room when you choose a topic for a research paper. This freedom can help you choose a topic you'll enjoy. (If your teacher has assigned something specific, you can still read the steps on "Do's and Don'ts" on the next page. There's often a way to personalize even the most specific topic. In addition, these guidelines will help you create a product you're proud of.)

Plan your project in the same way you'd plan any major project. (Review "Facing a Long-Term Project?" in Chapter 3.) Break the process into steps. The steps on the following pages will help you do this.

Plan how long you will spend on each step. Write the steps in your assignment book, working backward from the due date. Remember, though, to give yourself extra time at the end of the project, just in case you run into problems. As a general rule, plan to spend about one-third of your time writing.

Do's and Don'ts for Choosing the Right Topic

Think carefully about the research topic you choose. Finding an exciting topic will make your work interesting to you, and to your readers. Here are a few guidelines for choosing a topic that you'll enjoy—and learn from.

✓ Do

1. Write the assigned topic at the top of a piece of paper. Then brainstorm ideas for 15 minutes. Allow your mind to wander and write as many ideas as you can. At the end of 15 minutes, see what you have written. If nothing excites you, do something else for an hour, then brainstorm again.

2. Do some research. If your teacher assigns a paper on the Vietnam War, go to the library. Look at some books on the subject and see what sounds interesting.

3. Talk to a friend, a parent, or a teacher. Ask that person what he or she knows about the topic. A brainstorming session with your study group could also be useful here.

✗ Don't

1. Put the brakes on your imagination. Instead, write down all of your ideas, no matter how strange they seem. They may give you suggestions that you can use later.

2. Choose a topic that's so narrow you can't find enough information about it. Instead, make sure you can find several sources that contain different pieces of information about your topic.

3. Choose a topic that's so broad you can't possibly cover it well. For example, the topic "America in Vietnam" would be impossible to organize.

4. Choose a topic that's different from what your teacher assigned. If you have a question about your topic, clear your idea with him or her.

5. Choose a topic that doesn't interest you. This is important. There is probably *something* in the assignment that can interest you. A few minutes invested here will make all the difference in your attitude and your results.

Researching Your Topic

Chapter 6, "Becoming Resource Wise," gave you an overview of what's available at the library. Remember that you don't have to read whole books or magazines. You're looking for *specific information*. Check indexes and tables of contents for your subject. Then skim those pages to see if they have the information you need.

Here are a few ways to find resources outside the library.

- **Conduct interviews.** There may be people you know who could provide firsthand information about the topic you've

" Writing, like life itself, is a voyage of discovery. "

—Henry Miller,

writer

chosen. Find these people by asking your friends, your parents, your parents' friends, and groups that are concerned with your topic. You might also find that these people can suggest ideas for additional topics.

- **Talk to local organizations.** Your local Audubon Society may have pamphlets about birds. Local government agencies may have information on social services. A travel agency may have maps and pictures to add visual interest to a geography report. They may also be able to suggest local people who know about your topic. You can use these people as resources or as interview subjects.

- **Write to national groups.** They may be able to send you information sheets or other material.

All of these sources can provide information that is not available with just a quick trip to the library. They can add an extra dimension to your work. They can also show your teacher that you took an extra step to do a good job.

Taking Notes from Your Resources

Now you have a pile of books and articles. What do you do with it? First, get some index cards. Once again, they're handy tools. They will help you keep track of where you found each bit of information. They'll also help you prepare your footnotes and bibliography. (Pages 74–76 will give you more information on footnotes and bibliographies.)

Here are a few tips for organizing your research.

- On the top of an index card, write the name of the book along with the information you've found and the page number on which you found it. This will help you find your source again if you need to check your notes or add more information.

- Make another card that has just the name of the book, the author, and publication information. You'll use this card for your bibliography.

- Limit the information on each card to one idea or subject. Your cards will be easier to shuffle when you organize your paper.

- Use only one side of each index card. It's easier to arrange your cards if you don't have to turn them over.

See page 71 for an example of how two of these index cards might look.

types of fossils

Ages of the Rocks, By Kay Green, p.25

many kinds of fossils. Whole plants are rare.
Often original material replaced by minerals.

telescope, invention of

"History of Space," Jay Meri, Newsbeat,
March 3, 1973, p.10

earliest known telescope invented in the
19th century, could see spots on the sun's
surface with it.

The Problem with Plagiarism

Plagiarism—copying someone else's work—is a form of stealing. Yet your teacher wants you to use several sources. How do you avoid plagiarism? You credit your sources.

Most research is built on other people's work. That's why authors refer to books and articles that other authors have written. Research helps you benefit from others' work while you draw conclusions of your own.

When you're writing a paper, here is what you need to give credit for.

- Facts that someone else discovered

- Someone's original theory or idea

- Research that proves a theory

- A direct, or indirect, quotation from a book

- A photograph, a graph, or a table

There are, however, some things you don't need to give credit for.

- Information that everyone knows, such as the fact that the sun rises in the east

- Sayings that are so much part of our culture that no one knows who said them, such as "a stitch in time saves nine"

- A conclusion you reach that you later find someone else has also reached

> " There are no dull subjects. There are only dull writers. "
>
> —H. L. Mencken,
>
> writer

How to Conduct an Interview

If you're going to interview someone for a paper (or for any other reason, such as an oral history), it helps to plan what you'll say. Here are some tips for conducting an effective interview.

- Prepare the person for the interview by telling him or her why you want to do the interview and what kinds of questions you'll ask. This will give the person time to remember interesting stories or details about the topic.

- Set up a time and place to meet. Make sure you ask for enough time to explore ideas that the person raises. Then arrive on time or even ahead of time. You'll both feel more relaxed.

- Before the interview, find out as much about the person as you can. Research will help you focus your questions and keep the interview on track.

- Write your questions ahead of time. Arrange them so that you ask the easiest questions first. That will help put the person at ease. Order your questions so they are likely to lead from one subject to the next.

- Although you want to have all of your questions answered, be flexible. The person may have interesting information you didn't know about. However, if he or she seems to be getting off the track, try to return to your topic gently by asking another question on your list.

- Consider tape-recording your interview. You'll make sure your quotations are accurate. You'll also be able to concentrate on your conversation, not your notes. Get permission before you start taping, though.

- At the end of the interview, ask your subject if you may talk with him or her again. You may want to ask a few more questions or check your facts.

- Thank the subject for his or her time. Offer to give him or her a copy of what you write.

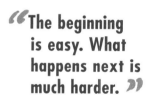

"The beginning is easy. What happens next is much harder. "

— Mavis Gallant, writer

What to Do With All That Information

You've now been researching for some time. You have piles of cards and no plan for dealing with them. It's time to take a breath and see what you have. Then you'll begin sorting your cards to see if you have what you need.

Sort the cards by topic. When you have them all sorted, look at the piles. Begin arranging them. What main points have you found? Which cards have details that support these main points?

Now think about your original idea. Is it working out or do you need to discuss a new direction with your teacher? If your research supports your main idea, it's time to make a rough outline of what you have. Arrange your cards so that you have your major points in different places. Then group the supporting information with the points they support.

Now write what you have in outline form. Find out if you need more information to support your topic. Make a list that will guide your final research.

Make Your Final Outline

Use your rough outline and your new research to make a more formal outline. As you construct this outline, be sure that your major points illustrate or prove the topic of your paper. Also make sure that you have details, examples, and facts to support each main idea in your outline.

The First Draft

Now you're ready to write your first draft. Stack your index cards in order, put your outline in front of you, and begin. Some people start with the first sentence. They write the introduction and thesis sentence, which is where you tell the point of the paper. These students find that writing this introduction helps sharpen their thinking.

Other people begin with their first point and write until they reach the end of the body. Then they write the introduction. These people say that sometimes what they think they'll write in an introduction changes. If they write the introduction last, they're sure it fits the body of the report.

Finally, write your conclusion. Your conclusion should restate what you said in your introduction.

In a Nutshell . . .

- Your introduction should tell what you are going to prove.
- The body of your report should contain your main points and your support for these points.
- Your conclusion should tell what you just wrote.

The Second Draft

Review what you wrote. Look for clarity and sense. Make sure that you proved your main points. Check that your details, facts, and examples are lively and interesting, and that they prove your main points.

Check your grammar, punctuation, and spelling. Finally, refer to the Chapter Checkup for Chapter 8, on page 67. Edit your paper, rewrite it, and take another look. If you're still not satisfied, go the extra step and recopy it.

Footnotes and Endnotes

Footnotes and bibliographies are the backbone of research papers. Whole books have been written about how to cite sources in works. The best-known is the *MLA Handbook*, which probably is available in your library. For most school work, you only need to know the basics. Here they are.

1. Use a footnote or endnote when you cite a source, quote someone, use an idea from someone else, or quote numbers or statistics. A footnote appears at the bottom of the page on which you quote the source. If the information is at the end of the paper, it is called an *endnote*. Both footnotes and end-notes contain the same information.

2. When you include a footnote or endnote, use a raised num-ber (called a *superscript*) at the end of the information you're using. Number your footnotes or endnotes in order through-out your paper.

3. Use the superscript number again at the beginning of the source information in the footnote or endnote.

Here are the usual forms for footnotes or endnotes.

A book:
Jane Jackson, <u>After the War</u>, (New York, Shanan Press, 1996), p. 39.

A magazine article:
Peter B. Neir, "The Harlem Experience," <u>Historical News</u>, March 1995, p. 22.

A newspaper article:
"African American Poet," by Kelcy Argo, <u>Bedford Chronicle</u>, July 17, 1993.

An article from an encyclopedia:
"Harlem Renaissance," <u>The Concise Columbia Encyclopedia</u>, 1983 ed., p. 202.

Bibliography

Use the index cards on which you've written your sources to make your bibliography. Add it to the end of your research paper. A bibliography should list all of the sources you used when you wrote your paper.

Some teachers also want to see the sources you used for general information, but did not quote. Here are general rules for creating your bibliography.

1. Write the entries in alphabetical order by author. If there is no author, alphabetize the work by the title.

2. Don't number the entries.

3. Begin each entry at the left margin. Following lines should be indented five spaces.

4. Leave a line space between each entry.

5. If you are using a number of works by the same author, write the author's name only for the first entry. After that, it looks like this:

> <u>Life and Times</u>. New York: Simon and Schuster, 1992.

Here are the different ways to cite sources in your bibliography.

With one author:
Honey, Ann. Believe the Animals. Boston: Dawson & Robert, 1990.

With two authors:
Honey, Ann and Ralph Floro. The Boston Tea Party. Boston: Dawson & Robert, 1988.

With no authors, only an editor:
Gibson, Mary, ed. A History of the South. New York: Franklin Pierce, 1992.

A story or an article from a collection:
Beck, Hillary. "The Forget-Me-Knot." In The Best 100 Stories Ever. New York: Jordon Publishing Co., 1993.

A newspaper or magazine article:
Clark, Bill. "The Cure for the Cities." Knoxville Planner, 12 Jan, 1990, p. 1.

If no author or editor is listed:
"New Thoughts." Dallas Times, 18 March, 1997.

In an encyclopedia, almanac, or other book of facts:
"Boston Tea Party." Settlement Encyclopedia. 1990 edition, p. 87.

Clued In

The Small Things That Add Up to a Great Grade

You can make your research paper look professional and improve your grade if you follow these tips.

- **Make sure you follow your teacher's instructions carefully.** If he or she wants the paper double-spaced, do it. If he or she assigns endnotes instead of footnotes, make sure that's what you do. It's surprising how often students stop listening and miss the details that make the difference.

- **Hand in your paper on time.** Some teachers subtract as much as a letter grade for every day a paper is late. You can avoid this trap by planning your time.

- **Triple-check your paper for spelling, grammar, and punctuation errors.** You want the teacher to focus on what you have to say, not on small errors. If you feel unsure of your ability to check, get a friend to help you.

- **Number the pages.** It makes your work look professional.

Did you know
?

Do you feel
as if you'll never
get that paper written?
Consider Pliny the Elder, who
lived in the first century A.D.
He wrote a 31-volume history
of Rome, a 27-volume history
of Roman warfare, a 37-
volume encyclopedia of natural history, an 8-volume Latin
grammar, and a 6-volume
guide to giving speeches.

- **If possible, type your paper.** It's amazing how much better typed words look than handwritten ones.

- **Double-space your paper, unless your teacher tells you otherwise.** If you use a computer, use a typeface such as Times Roman that is easy to read. Make sure the type is large enough to read (11 or 12 points) and that your margins are about 1 to 1½ inches on each side.

- **Make a copy, just in case.** You never know if the dog's really going to eat it.

- **Create an attractive cover page.** It should have the title of your paper, your name, the class, and the date. Here are some ways to arrange a cover page.

CHAPTER CHECKUP

The next time you have to write a research paper, use this checklist to make sure you're headed for success.

Topic
✓ I've chosen a topic that I'm interested in and that is not too large or too small.

Resources
✓ I've kept track of my sources by writing one source on each index card.
✓ I've written the book's title, author, call number, publisher, and date and city of publication on each source index card.

Organization
✓ I've used one card for each piece of information, with the title, author, and pages I used.
✓ I've sorted my cards and arranged them in piles with similar ideas.
✓ I've written an outline of the paper.

Writing
✓ I've written a first draft.
✓ I've revised my work, checking for sense, clarity, word usage, spelling, punctuation, and grammar.
✓ I've turned in a neat final copy, which I've triple-checked for errors, and typewritten, if possible.

Now think about what you learned in this chapter.

1. Why is your choice of topic so important when you're writing a research paper?

2. How can you avoid plagiarism?

3. List some general rules for making a bibliography.

CHAPTER TEN

Giving a Speech

Some people feel anxious just thinking of giving an oral report or speech. Does this describe you? If you follow the suggestions in this chapter, you'll feel more confident and you'll learn to prepare well enough to make a successful oral presentation. In this chapter, you'll learn

- The different kinds of speeches and how to give each one.

- Steps to prepare for any speech.

- How to tell—or not tell—a joke in a speech.

- How to add excitement to your presentations.

- Tips for feeling more confident when you are speaking in public.

Why Are You Talking?

There are several reasons to give a speech. Figuring out which one applies can help you plan an effective speech. Here are the main kinds of speeches you may be asked to prepare.

- **The informative speech.** Most of the speeches you will be asked to present will be informative speeches. Informative speeches tell your listeners something they don't know. This kind of speech is similar to a research paper. Organize your ideas so they flow from one main point to the next. You should have examples and details that support these main points. Informative speeches can explain something, report on something, or describe something.

- **The demonstration speech.** Demonstration speeches also tell your listeners something they didn't know. In a demonstration speech, though, you tell your listeners how to do something. You might give a demonstration speech on how to cook an eggroll or perform a science procedure. You explain things step by step, so your audience can follow and understand the procedure. Often, demonstration speeches require props so you can both show and tell your audience how to do something.

Did you know?

According to the *Guinness Book of Records*, the shortest inaugural speech in the United States was given by President George Washington in 1793, at his second inauguration. The speech lasted 90 seconds.

- **The persuasive speech.** Most speeches given by politicians are persuasive speeches. People who give persuasive speeches usually want to win their listeners over to their point of view. They may also want to urge their listeners to action.

- **The entertaining speech.** Stand-up comics give entertaining speeches. Featured speakers at banquets often give entertaining speeches. These speeches often include funny stories about others or about the speaker.

Who Is Your Audience?

As you read in Chapter 8, "The Art of Writing," it's important to know who your audience is when you're writing. It's also important to know who your audience is when you're preparing to give a speech.

Imagine you were scheduled to give a speech about saving the wolf to ranchers who think the wolf is threatening their livestock. You'd give a speech that is different from a speech you'd give to a group of environmentalists. Whenever you give a speech, find out about your audience. You'll be better able to use arguments that will convince your listeners.

Clued In

Watch a Pro

Pick up some clues from effective public speakers. First, think of teachers who hold your interest. You can also find a speaker on TV. Try to identify *how* that person keeps you listening. Keep notes while you watch.

- How does the speaker grab your interest?

- How does the speaker tell you when an important point is coming?

- How does the speaker move from one topic to another?

- How does the speaker use his or her voice for emphasis?

- How does the speaker use body language?

- What kind of ending does the speaker use?

- What do you remember from the speech? Did you understand the speaker's main points?

Planning and Giving Your Speech

Many of the same rules apply to giving speeches as to writing papers. With both assignments, you need to prepare carefully. You need to choose a topic and learn about it so that you can communicate something about it to your audience.

Choose Your Topic Carefully

Sometimes you won't have a choice. Your teacher may ask you to speak about a topic that doesn't excite you. If that's the case, look for some aspect of the topic that interests you. If you can choose a topic, pick a subject you enjoy. Chances are that your audience will enjoy it, too.

Research and Organize as if You Were Writing a Paper

See Chapter 9, "Writing a Research Paper," for information on how to research your topic. Even if it's an entertaining speech, you may need to do some research.

Write an Outline

Outlining, too, is discussed in Chapter 9. Make sure you have an introduction, a body, and a conclusion in your speech. For each main point, make sure you have supporting details. Depending on your purpose, there are several ways to organize your speech.

1. **Organize your speech by main points or topics.** In this style, you cover several different areas that are related to your subject.

2. **Organize your speech by chronology, or time order.** In this style, you talk about something such as a historical event in which events are best described in the order in which they happened.

3. **Organize your speech by problem solving.** In this style, you pose a problem and then talk about possible solutions.

4. **Organize your speech step-by-step.** In this style, you explain how to do something, such as assembling an electric motor.

Did you know?

Polish actress Helena Modjeska was known for her dramatic style of speaking. At one dinner party where the guests didn't speak Polish, she gave a dramatic reading in Polish that had her audience in tears. She recited the Polish alphabet.

Grab Your Listeners' Attention

"Be confident that you can make a difference. "

— Marian Wright
Edelman,
lawyer

It's important to interest your audience at the beginning of a speech. Whatever you say, you want your listeners to pay attention to you. You can do this in several ways.

1. **Tell an anecdote, or amusing story that makes a point.** This story can be about you, about someone you know, or just a story you heard. By telling an anecdote, you get your audience involved in your topic. The anecdote, of course, should deal with the topic of the speech.

2. **Say something surprising.** In the earlier example of a speech about wolves, imagine how a group of environmentalists might react to this beginning: "Wolves have no right to be here. Every one of them should be killed." Now you have your listeners' attention. You can go on to tell them that this statement reflects what many ranchers think.

3. **Tell a joke.** If you have just the right joke, it can make a great opening. But telling a joke is harder than it seems. Finding a joke that relates to your topic is tricky. If you do decide to tell a joke, be sure you don't offend anyone and that everyone will understand your joke. If you have the perfect joke and you've tried it out on friends who laughed, great. Otherwise, try a different kind of opener.

4. **Mention something your listeners didn't know.** You can sometimes start a speech with a fact that causes your audience to start thinking about your topic. That's a great way to begin.

5. **Connect your opening to your audience.** "If you're like me, you've always wondered . . ." is an example. Tell the audience why your topic matters to them.

Did you know?

Demosthenes, who lived about 350 B.C., was one of the best speakers of all time. He didn't start out that way, though. He stuttered as a child but trained himself not to stutter by putting pebbles in his mouth and practicing speeches.

Stay Lively

Remember that in a speech, even more than in a paper, you have to make sure you're holding your audience's attention. Keep your sentences short. The most effective spoken sentences have fewer than 20 words. If you use statistics, use only your best ones. Use lively words. Use the active voice. ("It was done by Jim" doesn't have the punch of "Jim did it.")

Use Clue Words

Help your audience. Use words that signal what you're going to say. Think about when you're listening to your teacher. The words such as "There are three ways to . . ." or "To sum up . . ." signal that you should pay attention.

Use Appropriate Visuals

Visuals can be tricky. Too many photographs or charts can distract your listeners. Use just a few carefully chosen visuals to show your audience what you mean or to add to your speech.

Write a Quick, Effective Conclusion

A conclusion should be short. It should signal that the speech is almost over. You could say, "I think you now see that. . . ." You could tell another anecdote that sums up your point. You could also make it clear in other ways that you're reaching the end.

Pause for a second. Raise your head and look at your audience. Your conclusion should leave your listeners with a quick overview of your main points. If you're speaking to persuade, the people listening should want to rise up and do what you tell them to do.

Know Your Time Limit—and Use It

At least some of your grade may depend on this, so be careful. Time yourself or have a friend time you. Then stick to the limit.

Your teacher has chosen the time limit for several reasons. As with a writing assignment, length guidelines will give you clues about how broad your topic should be. They will also tell you how much detail about your subject your teacher wants you to include.

What to Do While You're Standing There

Giving a speech can be frightening. Many teachers, though, and many jobs require that you speak to groups of people. Here are some tips for making you a more confident speaker.

- **Make cards to remind you of your main points.** You should write out your speech first, but it's easier to keep your place on index cards than on sheets of notebook paper. Number your cards. Write a main point in capital letters or

BETTER LUNCHES

HIRE A NEW COOK

MORE CHOICES

STUDENTS DESERVE A VOICE IN DECISIONS

" **The right word may be effective, but no word was ever as effective as a rightly timed pause.** "

— Mark Twain,
writer

in darker ink on each card. List the details and examples that support each main point on that card. Then practice your speech so that you know it well. Your cards should serve only as reminders.

- **Use body language.** Use your arms to gesture. Make eye contact with your audience. Pretend you're having a conversation with one person. Smile. Some people find it useful to concentrate on one person in the audience and talk directly to that person.

- **Use your voice.** Raise your voice slightly to make a point. Change the speed and pitch of your voice. Variety keeps an audience interested.

- **Pause.** Sometimes, silence can be very effective. Try it. Pause for a second to let an important point sink in.

- **Work on transitions.** Moving from one point to the next can be awkward. You can use a phrase to do this, such as, "Now, let me talk about. . . ." You can pause for three seconds to signal a change. You can also use body language. Change your position. Raise one hand to show that you're ready to make a new point.

- **Practice before a mirror, or have a friend videotape you.** When you practice, you become familiar with your topic. You'll find that soon you won't need to read your speech and you'll be less likely to lose your place. When you watch yourself either in a mirror or on tape, take notes about what you need to change or improve.

Clued In

Fighting Fear

You've written and practiced your speech, but you're still uneasy. Here are some ways to fight the fear of speaking in front of others.

- **Practice, practice, practice.** The more comfortable you are with what you have to say, the better you'll feel about being up there. Practice giving your entire speech several times. Then practice in front of friends and family.

- **Think positive.** Remember that almost everyone feels stage fright. Even professional actors are anxious before a performance. Tell yourself you can conquer your fear.

- **Use the deep breath technique.** Close your eyes just before you go on and take a deep breath. Hold it in three seconds, then let it out slowly. You'll feel more relaxed.

- **Spend that nervous energy on quick activity just before your speech.** Stretch. Push your hands together as strongly as you can for 10 seconds. Focus your energy.

- **Talk to a friend or a person you know in the audience.** As you give your speech, imagine you're having a conversation with that person.

> **"I do not object to people looking at their watches when I am speaking. But I strongly object when they start shaking them to make certain they are still going. "**
>
> — Lord Birkett, politician

CHAPTER CHECKUP

Grade yourself on your preparation for your next speech. You can also have a friend grade you. For each item, give yourself 0 points if you don't do it at all, 1 point if you do it somewhat, and 3 if you do it well.

To get ready for my speech, I

✓ Know the purpose of my speech.

✓ Know my audience.

✓ Research my topic.

✓ Write an outline for my speech.

✓ Use an audience-grabbing introduction.

✓ Keep my speech lively.

✓ Use a brief, memorable conclusion that states my main points.

✓ Use visuals that add to the presentation, if they are necessary.

✓ Write my main points on index cards.

When I practice my speech, I

✓ Use body language to make the speech interesting.

✓ Plan how to move from point to point.

✓ Practice enough so I know my speech well.

✓ Use my index cards only to help me find my place in a speech.

✓ Practice in front of a mirror or tape-record my speech.

✓ Practice at least once before an audience.

Are you ready? If your score is 0–20, keep working—hard. If you score 20–36, you would do better with more work. If you score 36 or higher, you're ready to speak.

Now think about what you learned in this chapter.

1. Briefly describe an effective speech that you gave or that you heard someone give. Why was the speech effective?

2. List three things you can do to control your fear before you give a speech.

UNIT 3

Studying in Subject Areas

CHAPTER ELEVEN

Language Arts

Language arts classes usually have two major topics: the mechanics of writing and understanding literature. You probably write in almost every class, which is why there is so much writing instruction in this book. You may even read literature in other classes. This chapter will help you master both areas.

The Reference section at the end of this book will help you remember some language arts basics, including words that are often misspelled, grammar and punctuation rules, and proofreader's marks.

In this chapter, you'll also learn

- How to understand the different forms of writing.

- How to write fiction and nonfiction, including poetry, plays, short stories, essays, and book reports.

The Forms of Writing

Literature is the written work of a people. It includes short stories, novels, poems, drama, essays, biographies, and other forms of fiction and nonfiction writing. You'll probably read all of these forms either in school or in your life.

Whichever form you're reading, though, you'll understand and enjoy your reading more if you read *actively*. Active reading involves not just figuring out words, but also thinking about what you read. What's going on? Why are the characters acting in this way? What does the writer want me to know? What does the writer want me to do?

There are guidelines throughout this book for reading actively. Here are some guidelines on how to actively read each form of writing you'll find in language arts classes and an outline of the important features of each form.

Fiction and Drama

Fiction and drama are created by an author. He or she may base a story on something that really happened or find inspiration in a newspaper article. An author can also use actual characters or events, but add fictional characters or events around them. Finally, an author can simply create a setting and characters that look like nothing on earth.

Short Stories. Short stories are short works of fiction. Usually, you can read a short story in one sitting. There are likely to be only a few characters and one main plot line. Every character and detail in a short story should work together to create one effect.

Novels. Novels are longer works of fiction than short stories. Often, novels have many more characters and a more complex structure. There may be a main story and several subplots. While every character and detail should work together, some elements can be more closely related to the main plot than others.

Drama. A drama, or play, tells a story through the actions and dialogue of the actors and actresses on a stage. The actions move the plot along, while the dialogue tells the story.

In addition to the words that the performers speak, plays have stage directions. Stage directions tell the performers where to be or how a character's voice might sound. Other stage directions deal with matters such as setting and mood (usually through lighting).

> ❝There are three rules for writing a novel. Unfortunately, no one knows what they are. ❞
>
> —W. Somerset Maugham,
>
> writer

Active Reading in Fiction and Drama: The Major Elements

There are four main elements in fiction and drama: plot, setting, characters, and theme. If you pay attention to each element while you read, you'll understand your reading more clearly.

Plot. What happens—the story—is the plot. Almost every plot revolves around a problem, or conflict. Most fiction and drama begin by introducing the characters and the situation to the audience. Then the problem, or conflict, is introduced. Next, there is the rising action followed by a climax, in which the problem reaches its highest point. Then, there is the falling action, in which a resolution is begun. Finally, the characters resolve the problem and the work ends.

Setting. When you read about a dark and stormy night on a deserted beach, that's the setting. It's the time and place in which the action occurs. The time may be the past, present, future, or a time that never existed. The place may be the corner drugstore or Mars. In some works, the setting is well defined. You can even place the street. In other works, the setting is left for the reader to imagine.

Characters. The characters are the people (or sometimes animals or alien beings) in a work of fiction. They move the plot forward. In a longer work, there often are main characters around whom the action centers and minor characters about whom we know less. Minor characters help tell the story.

Theme. The theme is why the writer has written this work. Most writers create novels, dramas, or short stories to say something about life. The theme could be "People can control their future" or "If people don't take care of the earth, they will destroy it." The theme is the writer's reason for telling the story.

What's Happening?

When you read a short story or a novel, ask yourself these questions as you read. They'll help you make sure you've understood the story and what the author was saying.

✓ What is the action of the story? (plot)

✓ Who are the people or other beings in the story? (characters)

✓ Where does the action take place? (setting)

✓ What is the author saying? (theme)

> **❝Fiction is obliged to stick to possibilities. Truth isn't. ❞**
>
> —Mark Twain,
> writer

Active Reading in Fiction and Drama: The Minor Elements

There are other elements in fiction and drama that help make them entertaining. If you look for these elements when you read, you'll gain a greater appreciation for literature.

Point of View. This is the voice in which a story or novel is told. There are three points of view. A *first-person* story is told from the narrator's perspective. In these stories, "I" tells the story. In a first-person narrative, you only know what the narrator knows.

There are two kinds of third-person points of view. In the *third-person-limited* point of view, a narrator tells what he or she sees. In the *omniscient* point of view, the narrator knows everything that happens. This may include knowing what the characters are thinking.

Mood. The mood is the feeling you get when you read a work. The writer can create details, setting, and plot events that make you feel happy or terrified.

Figurative Language. Writers use figurative language to create an effect. One type of figurative language is *hyperbole,* in which a writer exaggerates to make a point: "Matt's ego was as big as a house." A *simile* makes a comparison using *like* or *as*: "Andrea is as pretty as a picture." A *metaphor* also compares things, but does not use the words *like* or *as*: "The raindrops were tiny needles." A writer may also use *personification*, which gives human qualities to plants, animals, and other nonhuman objects: "The rock got its revenge by falling on the man."

Poetry

Poetry is written in lines that are meant to be read aloud. Because poems are usually much shorter than plays and novels, every word counts.

Poets write to describe something, to tell how they feel about something, or to explain something from a specific point of view. Poets can also tell a story. Many ancient works, such as *The Odyssey*, by Homer, are long stories told in poetic form.

Some poetry follows no regular form. This poetry is called *free verse*. Other poetry follows specific rules in form, rhythm, and rhyme.

Form. Poets write in lines that can vary in length. These lines are often arranged in groups, called *stanzas*. A space appears between stanzas.

Rhythm. The pattern of stressed and unstressed beats in a poem is its *rhythm*. Poetry may have a distinct rhythm, as in "There once was a young man from Kent." When you read this line aloud, you can hear that the stressed beats are on *once*, *young*, and *Kent*.

Rhyme. Some poems rhyme. Others don't. Poets who choose to rhyme words often use a pattern, called a *rhyme scheme*. A rhyme scheme may rhyme every pair of lines, which is expressed as *aabb*. A poet also could rhyme every other line, which is expressed *abab*. Other rhyme schemes are possible, too.

Active Reading in Poetry

There are several ways to read poetry actively. Here are a few.

- **Read the poem out loud.** Reading a poem aloud will help you understand what the poet had in mind when he or she

English writer Lewis Carroll, who wrote *Alice's Adventures in Wonderland*, invented some of the words he used in his books. Many of these words ended up in the English language. Two examples are *chortle* and *galumph*.

wrote it. To a poet, the way the words sound is often as important as what they mean.

- **Think about your reaction to the poem.** Poems are meant to give you a feeling and to make you see the world through the poet's eyes.

- **Give the poem a chance.** As you begin reading, keep your mind open. You don't have to like every poem you read, but you're more likely to enjoy your reading if you think positively. As you read, look for figurative language and mood, as well. (To review these elements, see "Active Reading in Fiction and Drama: The Minor Elements," on pages 90–91.)

Nonfiction

You will likely read different forms of nonfiction writing in your language arts classes. Some of the most common forms are biographies, essays, and accounts of real events told in story form. Here's how to recognize and appreciate each form.

Biography. A biography tells the story of a person's life. An *autobiography* is written by the person whose life is the subject. Some biographies begin at a person's birth and continue until the person's death. Others only discuss an important part of the person's life.

When you read a biography, pay attention to important events, facts, dates, and people in the person's life. Try to figure out why this person is important. Also think about the writer. What opinion does he or she want you to have of the person? You can tell how the writer feels about the person by the events and comments that are included and the way the writer comments on these events.

Essays. Essays give a writer's ideas or opinions about a person, issue, or event. An essay writer might describe the beauty of spring or the importance of rain forests.

Other essays try to change people's minds about an issue. An example might be an essay about the importance of recycling.

Essays often lead the reader through main points to a conclusion. As you read an essay, read actively. Try to guess why the writer included that fact. What is the next logical point?

Real-Life Stories. Real-life stories often sound like fiction, but they are true. True adventure stories are designed for interest and suspense—you want to know what will happen next. Usually, they move from the beginning to the end of the adventure.

When you read real-life stories, pay attention to setting. The characters often play off the setting, as in a story in which a person explores a cave alone. Character is another thing to consider. These stories usually tell of people's heroism. When you read a real-life story, ask yourself why the writer added that detail or what might happen next.

Language Arts Writing

Reread Chapter 8, "The Art of Writing," to review general writing tips. No matter what you're writing, it helps to sketch your ideas first, write a rough draft, then make a final copy. This section will help you apply these general rules to the specific forms of writing that you'll create in language arts classes. You may be asked to write nonfiction (an essay, autobiography, or biography) or to create a poem, short story, or play.

Review the first part of this chapter for hints about reading fiction, drama, poetry, and nonfiction. The elements that make an essay exciting to read also are useful in writing fiction. Here are some tips for creating the forms of writing you may be assigned in your language arts classes.

Nonfiction Writing

In nonfiction writing, you have to stick to the facts. Don't invent dialogue; write what people really said. You can get this information from firsthand accounts, such as interviews, or from your experience. Your opinions, and those of others, also count. So do the facts you choose to support what you say.

Essays. Much of the writing you'll be assigned will be essays. Essays are letters to the editor, letters to friends, and opinion pieces that tell how you feel about something. Book reviews are essays. Like research papers, essays need facts, details, and examples that support your ideas. Both essays and research papers also need the same elements. These elements include:

• An introduction, which tells how you feel.

> **"Your vision is not limited by what your eye can see, but by what your mind can imagine."**
> —Ellison S. Onizuka,
> astronaut

- A body, which proves why your opinion is right.

- A conclusion, which summarizes why you believe what you do.

Biography and Autobiography. If you start at the beginning of anyone's life and work through all of the details, you probably won't have your audience in suspense. Choose your details carefully.

Think of the points you want to make in your biography or autobiography. Does this person often help others? Does he or she have the spirit of a carefree artist? Choose a few stories that show what you want to say about the person. Then weave them together. If you have to do a complete life history of someone, include the facts, but link them with the stories that explain something important about the person's life (even if it's yours).

Tips for Terrific Book Reports

The next time you have to write a book report, try these tips.

- **Choose a book you want to read.** You'll be enthusiastic when you write about it. Ask a friend for a suggestion. Choose a kind of book you like (horror, science fiction, or romance). Read the back cover and inside front cover to see if you'd like to read further. Then read the first two pages of the book.

- **Take notes while you're reading.** Write things that interest you or that are well written or funny. Use these notes in your report to show why you liked (or didn't like) the book.

- **Look at book reviews in newspapers and magazines.** This may inspire you. You may find a new way of writing your report or something new to discuss.

- **Consider using another form of writing.** If your teacher agrees, a letter, a parody of the author's style, or a poster could offer a different slant on the assignment.

Creative Writing

For some people, creative writing is a snap. They seem to pluck ideas from the air. Most people, though, need some help getting started. Here are some tips for turning your ideas into finished work.

Poetry. Try these ideas the next time your teacher assigns a poem and you're looking for something to write about.

- Think of a strong emotion you had lately. Base your poem on that.

Rudyard Kipling, who wrote *The Jungle Book*, gave it to the nurse who had taken care of his newborn child. He thought she might be able to sell it later. Quite a few years later, the nurse did sell the book—and got enough money to live well for the rest of her life.

> I think that when a poem moves you, it moves you in a way that leaves you speechless. "
>
> —Rita Dove,
>
> poet

- Think of a place or person who means a lot to you. Write about that.

- Think of an event that made an impact on you.

- Look in books of poems to see what other poets have written about.

- Take a walk and bring a notebook along. You're bound to see something that gets you thinking.

Once you have a topic, try this technique for writing.

- **Brainstorm.** Write the words that describe what you want to write about.

- **Play with the words.** Add, subtract, and put words in different orders until they say what you want them to say.

- **Read what you've written out loud.** Reading aloud makes your work sound different. You can try other words to change the way your poem sounds.

- **Check your rhythm or rhyme.** If you're using rhythm or rhyme, try substituting different words to get the sounds you want in your poem.

Short Stories. Like novels, short stories have characters, a conflict that the characters resolve, and a theme that tells why the writer wrote the story. Details about the setting, characters, and events make the story come alive. How do you construct a story? Here are a few ways.

1. **Write a type of short story you enjoy reading.** If your teacher allows, consider mystery, adventure, science fiction, romance, or horror. Think about what each kind of story requires (horror, for example, requires a scary setting).

2. **Start by playing with ideas.** Instead of going right to paper, try imagining one of these things: characters who interest you, a setting you like, or a plot that contains a conflict. If you find yourself clicking with one element, keep going. A good start can make the assignment easier—and more fun.

3. **Read the newspaper.** If you're still stuck for ideas, try getting an idea from a newspaper story. Use a story about a dramatic fire rescue, for example, as the basis of a short story about two characters who must rely on each other to escape a fire.

4. **Write descriptions of your characters.** What might they do? How might they behave toward one another?

5. **Describe the setting.** When do your characters live? Where do they meet one another?

Literature helps us locate ourselves in the family, the community, and the whole universe. There's a power in words and stories to move and [change] us.

—Leslie Marmon Silko, writer

6. **Outline your plot.** Note what the conflict in the story might be and how the characters might resolve it.

7. **Now it's time for a rough draft.** Write it as it comes. You can always fix what isn't right when you revise. Don't worry about getting everything right the first time.

8. **Go back and revise.** Make sure you've chosen vivid words. Check that the plot makes sense. Is each of the characters described? Does the setting seem real? Do you like the way the story ends?

9. **Do a final check for mechanics.** Check over your spelling, grammar, and mechanics. Revise your work and you're done.

Drama. Having a good ear for language is a plus when you're writing drama. Knowing the form is another plus. If you are not familiar with plays, have one nearby to use for reference.

As you think about your play, review the main elements of fiction. Create a setting. Be sure you know your characters: what they look like, how old they are, what their backgrounds are. Think about the theme you're developing. Does the plot move forward and keep your audience interested? If you're having trouble creating a plot, try these ideas.

1. Turn a famous fable or well-known story into a play.

2. Use a dramatic event from your life or from the life of someone you know.

3. Create your characters first and then think about them. What might they say and do? What might cause them to disagree? How might they resolve this conflict?

4. Brainstorm with a friend. Sometimes it helps to bounce your ideas off someone else.

When you have an idea you like, write it in story fashion first. Then work on the dialogue. Check how it sounds by reading it out loud. If it doesn't sound like real speech, try again. When you finish the play, check that you have described the setting (or settings), listed the characters at the beginning, and included stage directions.

CHAPTER CHECKUP

Here are a few points to review before you do language arts home-work. Use the ones that relate to the work you've been assigned.

- ✓ What are the four major elements of fiction and drama?
- ✓ What are three examples of nonfiction?
- ✓ What are form, rhythm, and rhyme in poetry?
- ✓ What are three tips for writing great book reports?
- ✓ What are three ways to create ideas for poems?
- ✓ What are three ways to find possible plots for a play?

Now think about what you learned in this chapter.

1. Briefly describe a book, poem, or play you've enjoyed.
2. List three elements you found in that work.
3. How could you use these elements in your own writing?

CHAPTER TWELVE

Math

Are there ways to handle your math homework and to improve your performance in math classes? You bet. There are also tips for success on math tests.

The Reference section at the end of this book will help you remember some math basics, including metric measurements, algebraic formulas, and geometric shapes. In this chapter, you'll learn

- How understanding math can help you in other subjects and in the real world.

- How to get the most out of math class.

- How to make math homework count.

- Why you need to read math textbooks differently from other kinds of textbooks.

- How studying math is different from studying other subjects.

- Tips to help you answer test questions.

- Math problem-solving strategies.

- How to do mental math.

- How to quick-check math test answers.

Why Do You Need Math?

> **"People don't want technology, they want solutions to problems."**
>
> —An Wang,
> inventor

Many people who are successful in other subjects feel lost in math. Some people don't understand what they'll get out of math, except perhaps entrance to college. People who like math, of course, find this amazing. They love the logical way that numbers fit together and the constructions they can make with numbers. No matter which of these views you hold, though, there are lots of ways in which math is important in your life.

- Even if you're not a math teacher, you may need to borrow money, calculate the path of a sailboat, or figure your profit in your own business.

- In most jobs, knowing some math is essential. Accountants, carpenters, engineers, mechanics, secretaries, and doctors, for example, use math every day. For other jobs, people need to figure out budgets and costs of many kinds.

- Math can teach you how to think. It can teach you how to look at problems, how to take a step-by-step approach to solving them, and how to build on your knowledge to find a solution. There is also considerable creativity in math. Mathematicians rely on their instincts to make guesses that they then prove or disprove.

- Math can improve your powers of concentration. You have to think a problem through to its conclusion, often through many steps. This is good training for solving problems in all areas of life.

Getting the Most Out of Math Class

Math class is not the place to catch up on your sleep. Math concepts build on one another. If you lose track of what's happening in class, you may miss an important building block. That's the first rule. Go to class and pay attention. If you miss class, get the notes from a friend and make sure you understand them.

Before Class

Look over what the teacher will be discussing before you go to class. Pinpoint places that may give you trouble. If there is homework to do, make sure you do it—on time. If you do these simple things before class, you'll have made a leap toward understanding.

In Class

Here are a few tips for taking notes that you'll be able to understand later.

1. Keep a separate place in your notebook for math notes.

2. Write the date and the topic at the top of a piece of notebook paper. Then make sure to copy every problem your teacher writes on the board. What the teacher discusses is important. It's also a good clue to what to expect on a test.

3. Copy the problem exactly as it is on the board. Label it with whatever words the teacher uses.

4. Write down, step by step, how the teacher solves the problem. Leave room in the margins for additional notes.

5. Be careful about how you write notes. Write in clear, large numbers and letters. Leave space between problems so you can tell where one ends and the next one starts.

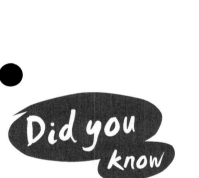

Did you know?

As I was going to St. Ives, I met a man with seven wives. Every wife had seven sacks, every sack had seven cats, every cat had seven kits. Kits, cats, sacks, and wives, how many were going to St. Ives? What is the answer to this ancient riddle? One.

After Class

When you get home, review the day's material. Do the problems again to see if you get the same result as the teacher.

If you're falling behind, take action. Schedule a session with your teacher. To make the time productive, pinpoint where you become confused. Circle the parts that you don't understand so you and your teacher can go right to the trouble spots.

Making Math Homework Count

To understand math, you need to be an active student. When you sit down to do your math homework, follow these tips in order.

1. **Review your class notes and the problems discussed in class.** Do the problems again to make sure you know the procedure. Circle what you can't figure out.

2. **Look over your textbook assignment.** (See "Active Reading in Math," below.) Do the sample problems. Don't start your homework until you've figured out these problems.

3. **Now do your homework.** Clearly show how you reached the answer to each problem.

4. **Use math aids.** Calculators and computers aren't magic, but they can be useful tools. Remember, though, that calculators and computers are only tools. If you don't know the correct steps to solve a problem, they won't do it for you.

5. **Review what you've learned before you put your work away.** Make sure you understand the steps. Now make up your own sample problems and solve them.

Clued In

Active Reading in Math

When you read a math textbook, it's very important to be an active reader. Talk back to your textbook. Here's how to start this "conversation."

- **Scan before you start.** You'll have a better idea of where you're going.

- **If you don't understand a problem or process, stop.** Figure out where you start losing the train of thought and concentrate there. As you've read, math concepts build on one another. If you don't understand a concept, try again or get help from a friend or teacher.

❝ Everyone can make a contribution, no matter who they are. ❞

— Portia B. Gordon,
pharmacologist

- **Pay careful attention to formulas, diagrams, graphics, etc.** Write this important information on an index card. Write the explanation on the back. Keep these cards for your review. Many math formulas should be memorized, too.

- **Talk back to your textbook by doing every sample problem.** Cover the answer, write the question, and then work it out. Check that you got the same results as the book. When you do this, you're an active reader—and learner.

- **If you don't get the same results as the book does, get help.** You could try finding another math textbook. Perhaps just reading a different explanation will answer your questions. In addition, you could see your teacher or your study group. Someone else in your class or an older brother or sister also could help you.

Taming Word Problems

"If a woman invested $50,000 for a year at 6% interest, and $20,000. . . ." When you see a word problem, do you feel nervous? Here are some ways to attack word problems.

1. Have you done a similar problem successfully? Review how you did it.

2. Circle the words and numbers in the problem that matter. Cross out those that don't.

3. Look at what the problem asks. What do you know? What do you need to find out? Write this information.

4. Once you have figured out what information you have and what information you need, you've done most of the work. Translate the problem into math symbols, such as an algebraic formula.

5. Use the information you need to estimate an answer.

6. Now try to solve the problem.

7. Check to see if your answer makes sense. If not, rethink your answer.

Do You Need a Math Test?

If you're having trouble keeping up and you feel frustrated, you may need a math tune-up. Ask your teacher for a basic math test to see if there are roadblocks in your understanding.

Take the test and score it yourself. Once you know where your problems are, your teacher can help you catch up.

Math Test-Taking Tips

Review Chapter 7, "The Art of Taking Tests." All of these rules apply to math tests, too. Here's a checklist that can help you improve your scores.

Before the Test

- **Carefully review your old quizzes and tests.** Look at the types of problems your teacher chooses and the number of problems that are on the tests. Notice how much of your work he or she wants you to show. Notice if your teacher has commented on your neatness—or lack of it.

- **Memorize the formulas that will be on the test.** Write each formula on an index card. Study the formulas until you feel like you know them. Then, have someone quiz you to make sure you know every one.

- **Practice working against the clock.** Be sure that you don't just do the problem, but that you do it correctly.

- **Practice doing different types of problems.** If you work on different types of problems, you won't find yourself saying: "But I didn't think that would be on the test!"

- **Make your own sample test.** Be sure to include all of the different types of problems that the test will cover. You could also review with your study group.

On Test Day

- Bring several sharpened pencils and an eraser.

- When you are given the test, look it over quickly to see what's ahead.

- Start with the sections you know best.

- Notice which items have the most points attached. Spend more time with them.

- Make sure you understand the directions. Read them twice and underline important words.

- If your teacher wants to see your work, provide it.

- Finally, be sure to check your work.

Math Problem-Solving Strategies

As you did in Chapter 3, put your learning style to work for you. Here are some techniques to try.

- If you learn best by seeing things, draw a picture. Make a sketch. This works well with some word problems.

- If you learn best by listening, talk through the solution. Tell yourself what you're doing. You could also talk problems through with a friend.

- If you learn best by doing things, make the problem concrete. For example, with geometry you can cut out shapes and move them around.

Guess and Check

This can be a good way to begin. Look at the problem. Round the numbers up or down to work with "easier" numbers. Work it through in your head. Then test your answer.

Now take another look. Adjust your figures. Work through the problem again and check your answer.

You can also use this technique when you have a multiple-choice math test. Choose one answer. Test it to see if it works. If it doesn't work, think about whether the number should be higher or lower.

Now, test another answer. Keep testing until you find the right choice.

Work Backward

Sometimes a teacher will give you part of a problem and ask you to work backward to find earlier numbers. For example, a word problem might read, "Susan and Brad sold $476 worth of vegetables at the Farmer's Market. Their profit is 10 percent of everything they sell. They sold $47 worth of onions and $121 worth of tomatoes. They sold the rest in herbs. What is their profit on herbs?"

If you work backward from $476, you'll find the answer. Subtract $47 and $121 from $476, and you get $308. That's how much was sold in herbs. Because the profit is 10 percent, you know they made $30.80 on herbs. You worked backward from the number $476 to find the answer.

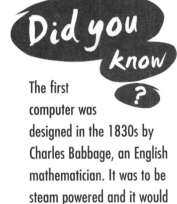

The first computer was designed in the 1830s by Charles Babbage, an English mathematician. It was to be steam powered and it would have worked. The problem was that the inventor had no money to develop it.

Make a Table, List, or Chart

Sometimes, particularly with word problems, it helps to draw a picture, make a graph or chart, or write a list. For example, if a story problem says, "Mary spent $46, Tim spent $30, Saul spent $50. Each had to spend an additional 8 percent for sales tax. How much. . . ." you might be make a chart like this:

Name	Amount Spent	Sales Tax (8%)
Mary	$46	$3.68
Tim	$30	$2.40
Saul	$50	$4.00

Look for a Pattern

Patterns can be helpful when you're searching for the missing piece in a problem. Look for the differences among the bits of information you have. Write the numbers or letters side by side and see how they are alike and how they are different.

Once you figure that out, you can fill in the missing pieces. Sequencing is one kind of problem in which this is useful.

Mental Math

Making reasonable guesses can help you get close to an answer in math. It will also be a handy skill throughout your life. Here are some ways to do mental math.

Round Those Numbers

Round to the nearest ten or hundred. The only trick is to remember to correct for the amount you've added or subtracted to round your numbers.

It's a snap to add 498 + 549 if you use rounding. Look at this example:

498 + 549 = ?

Round 498 to 500.	498 → 500 (−2 = 498)
Round 549 to 550.	549 → +550 (−1 = 549)
	1050 −3 = 1047

You can do the same thing when you're subtracting. Try subtracting 488 from 610. Now try it this way: Round 488 to 500. Round 610 to 600. Subtract 500 from 600, add 12 and then 10 more. That's a bit easier.

Multiply in Round Numbers

You can also round numbers when you multiply. Round to a number that you easily can use in your head. Multiples of 10 are easy to use. Once you choose a round number, multiply the smaller numbers that are left. For example:

47 × 14 = ?

Break 14 into 10 and 4.

Multiply 47 by 10.	47 × 10 = 470
Multiply 47 by 4.	47 × 4 = 188
Add the products.	470 + 188 = 658

Group Numbers by Place Value

If you're adding or subtracting, you can make things easier if you do it by ones, tens, hundreds, and so on. For example,

587 + 387 = ?

Add the hundreds.	500 + 300	= 800
Add the tens.	80 + 80	= 160
Add the ones.	7 + 7	= 14
Add the sums.	587 + 387	= 974

Clued In

Eight Ways to Quick-Check Your Answers

- Look at the question again. Does the answer make sense?

- Is your answer within a reasonable range? Is it close to your estimate?

- If the problem has several steps, quick-check each step. Are your results reasonable?

- Another tip for multi-step problems is to solve each part of the problem by itself. Then assemble the pieces.

- Create a problem that's similar but easier. Now check your answer. Does it make sense?

- If it's a geometry problem, check your work with a drawing or a grid.

- If it's a problem that involves a visual measurement or a graph, compare your answer with the graph. Does it make sense?

- Often, you can solve a problem using more than one method. If you have time, use the second method to check your work. Do you get the same answer with both methods?

CHAPTER CHECKUP

Do you use these tips when you study math and take math tests? Give yourself 1 point for each tip you use.

✓ Be prepared for class. Look over what your teacher will be discussing in class. Make sure you complete your assignments on time.

✓ Date your notes, list the class, and write the day's topic at the top of your notebook paper.

✓ Write notes that you'll be able to understand later. Include all of the steps you need to solve a problem. Leave enough room in the margins for more information.

✓ Review after each class and work some examples of the problems covered in class.

✓ Do the sample problems in the textbook.

✓ Don't go on to the next section until you understand the one you're working on.

✓ Ask your teacher or a friend for help if you're falling behind.

✓ Study for tests by working against the clock, reviewing the work on past quizzes, and making up and solving sample problems.

✓ Use a variety of problem-solving strategies: work backward, guess and check, make a table or picture, and look for a pattern.

✓ Know and use mental math.

✓ Know a variety of ways to quick-check your answers.

If your score is 8 or higher, you're on the road to success. If your score is below 8, reread this chapter and keep trying. Don't give up!

Now think about what you learned in this chapter.

1. List three steps you'll use to learn math actively.

2. How can you use your learning style to help you learn math?

CHAPTER THIRTEEN

Science

Science is the knowledge of how things work. For scientists, the thrill is in solving the puzzle. What kind of rubber makes the best tires? Can that plant be used to fight cancer?

Seen in the right light, science is a great adventure. With the information in this chapter, you can spend more time enjoying the exploration—and less time wondering what's going on.

The Reference section at the end of this book will help you remember some of the science basics, including the classification of organisms, the Periodic Table of the Elements, and the geological time line.

In this chapter, you'll learn

- The importance of the scientific method.
- How to get the most from science class.
- The secrets for studying a science textbook.
- How to handle science lab.
- Tips for different science topics.
- How to read charts and graphs.
- The best way to review for science tests.

The Scientific Method: The Basis of Science

> *What many scientists are after is the adventure of discovery itself.*
> —Sir Cyril Hinshelwood, scientist

The scientific method is a special way of asking and answering questions. When you do a lab experiment, you'll probably be asked to use the scientific method. This method of collecting and analyzing information can help you explain many things, including how volcanoes erupt and why some lizards change color. Here are the steps of the scientific method.

1. **Make observations.** Science begins with observing something and wondering about it. For example, you might notice that there are dead fish in a stream near a place where water is running off from the land.

2. **Identify and state the question.** Turn your observation into a question. Why did the fish die? It is important to choose the right question. If you choose a question that is too broad, it will be impossible to answer. You also have to be careful to choose a question that you have the resources to answer.

3. **State a hypothesis.** Your hypothesis is your possible answer to the question that you stated. If your hypothesis is that the fish are dying because of a worldwide condition, it may be difficult to prove. On the other hand, you may hypothesize that the fish are dying because of a poison in the runoff. Hypotheses are made in the form of a statement: "I think the fish are dying because a poison in the runoff is killing them."

4. **Design an experiment.** To design an experiment, you must first design a step-by-step plan. Anyone should be able to understand or repeat your experiment. This is important because science builds from one idea to the next. For the dead fish problem, you might test your hypothesis by testing the water upstream and downstream from the runoff to see if there are chemicals that are poisonous to fish.

5. **Keep a record of your data.** It is also important to keep careful records so that others can see exactly what happened in your experiment. Scientists record everything about their experiments, including the time of day and the place the data were collected and how they set up everything. These details help other scientists to repeat the experiment to see if the data can be applied to their own work.

6. **Organize and analyze your data.** Scientists organize their data. Tables, graphs, charts, and diagrams can organize and help explain data. The data can then be studied and analyzed more easily.

7. **State a conclusion from your data.** Look at all of your data to see what the information means. Then write your hypothesis and a sentence that will say either, "The data do not support the hypothesis" or "The data show that the hypothesis is correct." If the information you gathered does not support the hypothesis, you may need to find another hypothesis to test.

See the chart on the next page for an example of how one student kept notes on an experiment.

Getting the Most from Science Class

Many of the tips for science class are the same as for math class. There's a reason for this: The basis of many sciences is math. In science, as in math, if you don't understand a concept, you may miss what follows it. If you miss class, get the notes from a student who takes clear notes. Once you get to class, make sure you pay attention. Then try these tips.

- **Look over the material the teacher will be covering.** This means doing your homework and taking notes about what you find confusing. If you still don't understand them at the end of class, ask the teacher for help.

> *Research is the process of going up alleys to see if they are blind.*
>
> —Marston Bates, naturalist

SCIENTIFIC PROCESS

STEPS	NOTES
1. Make an observation.	Plants seem to need sunlight.
2. Identify and state the question.	Do plants need sunlight to live?
3. State a hypothesis.	I think plants need sunlight in order to live.
4. Design an experiment.	1. Buy 2 identical plants. 2. Place Plant 1 in sunlight and Plant 2 in closet. 3. Give both plants the same amount of water. 4. Check plants every other day. 5. Compare the 2 plants at the end of the week.
5. Keep a record of your data.	Day 1: Plant 1—bright green; Plant 2—bright green Day 3: Plant 1—bright green; Plant 2—dull green Day 5: Plant 1—bright green; Plant 2—edges of leaves brown Day 7: Plant 1—bright green; Plant 2—leaves brown and falling off
6. Organize and analyze your data.	after 1 week: Plant 1 is healthy Plant 2 is withered
7. State a conclusion from your data.	Plants need sunlight to live.

- **Date and number your notes.** Write the topic at the top of the paper. Write down formulas and facts that seem important. If your teacher writes something on the board, you should write it down, too. If the teacher stresses a concept, put an arrow next to it, underline it, or circle it in your notes.

- **Use those handy science abbreviations.** It's quicker to write "H_2O" than "water."

- **Everything connects to everything else in science.** Idea maps may help you take clearer notes because they help you see these connections. To make an idea map, write a main concept and circle it. Then write other concepts that are related and connect them to the main circle. This method of taking notes was discussed in Chapter 4, "Study Skills for Every Class." See pages 28–30 for a reminder.

- **These connections help you understand systems.** If you study connections instead of isolated facts, you'll remember how systems work. It's also easier to keep things in your memory if you can relate them to one another.

- **Be neat.** You won't be happy if you miss a formula because you think a B is an E.

- **When you get home, review.** Study the main concepts, the formulas, the details, and examples of each.

- **If you're falling behind, see your teacher right away.** Bring your notes. Show him or her exactly what's not making sense to you. Your teacher would rather help you before a test than after it.

Active Learning in Science

If you do your assignments on time, keep from falling behind, and use some of these tips, you'll do fine.

Here are a few techniques to help you learn science actively.

- **Survey your science book.** Check the back of your book for reference material. Often there are tables, graphs, charts, and other information that will help you understand the material. You can use the Reference section at the back of this book to quick check some science facts, too.

- **Scan the reading assignment.** Then read it. Write questions you think the text will answer, then answer the questions yourself. If you see something that puzzles you, stop. In science, as in math, you need to learn one concept before you tackle the next one.

- **Talk back to your textbook.** Read the information and ask questions. Look in your notes and your textbook for the answers.

- **Draw diagrams.** Diagrams can help you explain the information in another way. Write the concept in your own words. Respond to your notes. Make a drawing of a system or process and label it.

- **Use the book's glossary.** The glossary is the mini-dictionary in the back of your science book. Science books have glossaries because the words are often difficult, but important. When you find a word you don't understand, look it up. If the word isn't in the glossary, look in a regular dictionary.

Few people knew that the artist Leonardo da Vinci kept coded notebooks. These notebooks show that da Vinci understood how blood circulated, that the Earth was not the center of the universe, and how fossils formed—hundreds of years before anyone else did.

Make an index-card science dictionary. Write the word on one side and the definition on the other. Carry the cards around until you know the words. Use them for review when you study for a test.

- **Watch for graphics and tables.** Science is filled with facts, and many facts are shown in tables and charts. Science is also filled with processes. For example, a diagram can help you understand photosynthesis. A table can give you a quick review of an experiment's data. When you see graphics and tables in the text, pay attention. They probably contain useful information.

Science Lab Success

Doing lab work is a big part of many science classes. You'll get more out of it if you try these tips.

- **Know the procedure ahead of time.** You need to follow the rules precisely, but it's easier if you already know what to do. This way, when you get to the lab, you can concentrate on your results, not on how to find them.

- **Keep lab notes in a separate notebook.** You won't confuse your results with the information you need to study.

- **Follow the instructions exactly.** Write everything that happens. It's difficult to reconstruct an experiment if you don't take notes carefully.

Let the Real World Help You Out

Science is all around you. Put that to work for you. As you study, try the following suggestions.

- Relate the information to your everyday life. Think about a friend who witnessed a volcanic eruption. Think about how light looks when you study refraction.

- Make connections between your world, your classroom, and your textbook. You'll find it's easier to understand concepts and remember them when you can see them at work.

Different Words for Different Sciences

What physicists study is light-years (so to speak) away from what biologists study. All the sciences are related to one another, but they're also distinct. Understanding their differences can help you in science classes.

Biology. In biology, also called *life science*, classification is key. Biologists have placed most living creatures into their own

special category. Biologists look at the living things in the world in terms of their relationship to other living things and where they fit into that order.

Systems also are important in biology. There is a system for everything in your body, from your skin to your blood. Learn how these systems interact.

Earth Science. Many earth science activities rely on observation. Scientists often study land forms, resources, water, climate, weather, and space through fieldwork.

Earth science draws on the other branches of science as well. For example, astronomy is closely related to physics, and geology makes use of chemistry.

Chemistry and Physics. These sciences focus on matter and energy. They rely heavily on procedures. Understanding *why* you are doing things in a certain way is important. If you just memorize a procedure, you won't be able to adapt or change it easily.

Also, keep in mind that much of chemistry and physics is built on math, particularly algebra. If this is stopping you, get help. Often, science textbooks contain reference pages that can help you understand the math behind the science. (Review the guidelines for actively learning from math textbooks in Chapter 12.)

Getting the Most from Graphs and Tables

Scientists use graphs and tables to chart results from experiments and to illustrate how data can help lead to a conclusion. To do well in science, you need to know how to read these graphics.

Line Graphs

Line graphs chart information through points on a line. Then the points are connected to show change, often change over time. The vertical axis may show measurements such as feet or populations. The horizontal axis may show things such as different years.

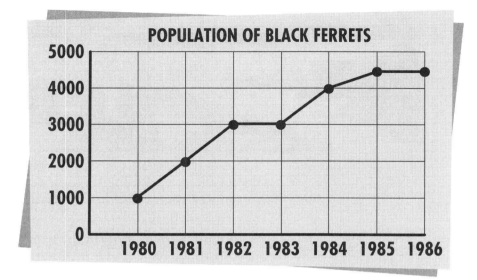

> " When I was a kid, I wanted to know what made it all work. I looked at the shapes of the mountains and the rocks, and I wondered how they got that way. "
>
> —Fred Begay,
> physicist

Bar Graphs

Bar graphs can help you compare facts. The items on the horizontal axis are each represented by a single bar. The items on the vertical axis may show numbers or years.

While a line graph can show how one thing changed over time (how a population of black ferrets changed over a 6-year period), a bar graph is better able to show how individual items fared (how different kinds of animal populations compare to one another.)

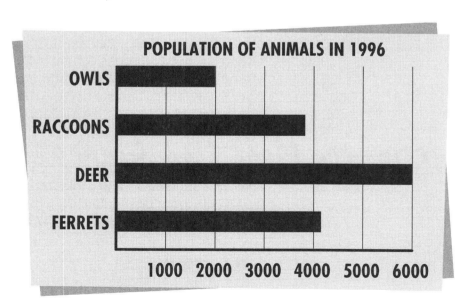

Pie Charts

Pie charts show how a whole is divided. You might see a pie chart that analyzes the percentage of different kinds of minerals and chemicals in a soil sample or a series of pie graphs that show how people moved to cities over a number of years.

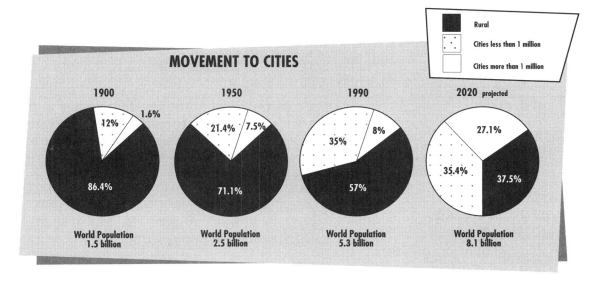

Data Tables

Scientists often use tables to record information. You have probably used them yourself in science experiments. Data tables can help you record information and make sense of it. For example, if you are recording temperatures every four hours for three days, it is much easier to organize and understand the information if you put it in a data table.

TEMPERATURE FOR WEEK OF NOV. 10–17

	MON.	TUES.	WED.	THURS.	FRI.	SAT.	SUN.
1 AM	51	49	40	40	50	43	44
4 AM	50	49	40	41	49	43	42
7 AM	54	52	47	50	51	47	44
10 AM	57	48	49	60	54	50	48
1 PM	64	66	39	54	70	54	55
4 PM	60	66	38	53	71	52	53
7 PM	54	59	38	50	66	54	50
10 PM	50	45	38	48	54	50	48

There are several sets of index cards you should create as part of your science course.

- **Vocabulary cards.** Write the word or phrase on one side and the definition on the other side.

- **Theory cards.** Write theories and laws on one side and the explanation and an example on the other side.

- **Formula cards.** Write formulas on one side and the explanation and an example on the other side. Even in biology courses, there are scientific and mathematical formulas on which understanding the material is based.

These cards are the basis for your review, along with past tests, your homework, and your notes. But because science is filled with relationships, connections, and systems, you need to go beyond knowing the isolated information on each card.

Once you have the information you need written on cards, try these tips for science success.

- **Sort your cards into systems.** This process will show you how the information is connected. How does a formula apply to a theory? How do the pieces work together to form systems? You can probably use some cards in several systems.

- **Study old tests.** What kinds of questions does your teacher tend to ask? Does he or she use essay or multiple-choice tests?

- **Make up your own test.** Make up tests with a friend or with your study group and exchange tests. Then study the points that aren't clear.

- **Have a parent or a friend quiz you.** You'll be sure you can explain the information you've gathered.

> **The scientific theory I like best is that the rings of Saturn are composed entirely of lost airline luggage.**
>
> —Mark Russell,
> humorist

CHAPTER CHECKUP

How many of these things do you do when you're studying science?
Give yourself a point for every one you do.

Basic Science Understanding

✓ Know and understand the seven steps of the scientific method.

✓ Understand the importance of systems and classification in biology.

✓ Know the math that you need to do the science.

Preparation for Class

✓ Review your notes for science class ahead of time and complete all assignments on time.

✓ Read and understand the procedures before you go into science lab. Once you're in the lab, take careful notes of everything you do.

✓ Keep index cards of science words, concepts, formulas, and ideas that are central to understanding the topic. Divide your cards into systems and topics to understand how the pieces relate to the whole.

✓ Pay attention to graphics, tables, and charts in the text and in class. Know how to make them yourself.

✓ Scan the back of the textbook for the glossary and reference pages, and use them.

✓ Don't go on until you understand what you're studying. Get help if you're lost.

Preparation for Tests

✓ Make up your own test to study or trade tests with another student.

✓ Have a parent or friend quiz you.

If you scored 0–3 points, reread this chapter. If you scored 4–7, you're on your way. If you scored 8–11, keep up the good work.

Now think about what you learned in this chapter.

1. List three steps you'll use to learn science actively.

2. How can knowing the scientific method help you succeed in science class?

CHAPTER FOURTEEN

Social Studies

Social studies is the story of how and why people do things. It's drama and it's the stories of people's lives. It includes you and everyone you know.

The Reference section at the end of this book will help you remember some of the social studies basics, including the presidents of the United States and the states and their capitals. It also includes maps of the Eastern and Western hemispheres. In this chapter you'll learn some hints for making social studies more exciting. You'll also learn

- How to get more out of social studies studying.

- Time line tricks.

- Propaganda and code words and how to spot them.

- How to test for the truth.

- The difference between primary and secondary sources.

- Several ways to write social studies essays.

- How to read many different kinds of maps.

Points of View

People can view the same event or idea in history in many different ways. Recognizing a speaker's point of view is important in judging if a book or article is a reliable source of information.

Here are two different points of view about the study of history. How are the speakers' views different? Why might two people have such different views about what people can learn from the past? What do you think you can learn from the past?

"We are tomorrow's past."

—Mary Webb,

writer

- "American history is longer, larger, more various, more beautiful, and more terrible than anything anyone has ever said about it."—writer James Baldwin

- "History is little more than the register of the crimes, follies, and misfortunes of mankind."—historian Edward Gibbon

Active Learning in Social Studies

The tips in Chapter 3, "Studying Better," apply directly to social studies classes. Here are some additional tips to help you learn actively in social studies.

- Many people improve their understanding of social studies by studying with a map. If you can, make a copy of a map of the area you are studying and mark places you read about. Make notes on index cards of major events or characters as you read.

- If the section is about a period of time, make your own time line as you read. Mark the date and write both the event and a little about it. (See page 120 for more information on making time lines.)

- Think, "What is the point of this? What is the author, or my teacher, trying to tell me?" Most history is presented in themes. Your teacher will help you identify these themes. Themes could include the impact of the Industrial Revolution on England or of the Black Plague on the Middle Ages. Then look for connections with that theme as you read or listen in class.

- Look at history from the point of view of a reporter. Think of the Five Ws: Who, What, Where, When, and Why. Apply this information to your reading. It will help you understand the whole story.

- As you make your index cards for social studies classes, write an important event, person, place, or theme on the front of the card and the description on the back.

Five Ways to Make Studying History Fun

1. **Think about historical figures as real people.** Go beyond the textbook and find out more about these people's dreams, quirks, and blind spots.

2. **Make a connection to something in your life.** Often, you can read about what someone did and wonder what he or she was thinking. First, think about what *you* might have done. How might you have solved this problem differently? Second, put yourself in the shoes of the person making the decision. What information did he or she know, or not know, that led the person to that decision? Playing "what if" with history can give you new insights..

3. **Watch television documentaries and movies about events in history.** Ken Burns's series on the Civil War is one example. Find out what videos your public library has available for checkout or for watching there.

4. **Read biographies.** A good biography tells you not just about the person, but also about the times in which he or she lived. You'll find out about such things as the ideas and recreations of the times.

5. **Read fiction about the subject.** A good historical novel can bring history alive. Ask your teacher or librarian for suggestions. You'll impress your teacher with your extra effort and learn things that make the facts take on new interest.

Clued In

Time Line Tips

Making your own time line can be very useful. Here's a mini-lesson in how to do it.

1. Scan what you are studying. Note the beginning and ending dates.

2. Put the beginning date on the far left and the ending date on the far right of a line.

3. On the top and bottom of the line, write information about the dates as you read.

4. Dates that are very important can be highlighted or underlined. You can also stagger information, as is done in the time line below.

5. This kind of ordering gives you a visual record of what's important and when it happened. It can be a great aid when you're studying.

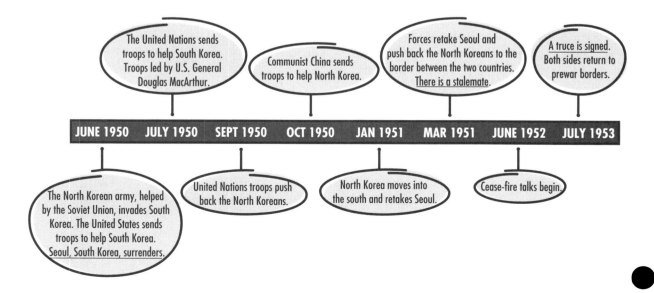

Would You Trust This Person?

Propaganda is one tool that both dictators and advertising copywriters use. They try to persuade you to think or act in a certain way. How can you be alert for the truth? Try this Nonsense Detector on the next ad you see or the next political speech you hear. Mark the techniques you see in action.

- **Don't miss out!** These appeals try to get you to think that unless you act now, you'll miss something fabulous. A variation of this, also called *jumping on the bandwagon*, is for a writer to say that "everyone" believes something. If you don't, you're missing something terrific—right?

- **Expert, expert.** When you hear that an "expert" believes something, put up your radar. Can you trust this expert, or are you supposed to believe it just because the writer or speaker said so?

- **I'm just like you.** This is an attempt to tell you that you and the speaker are alike. Because you are alike, it's natural for you to identify with, and believe, the speaker.

- **Connect with good feelings or nostalgia.** "Remember the days when there was a chicken in every pot and you were young and happy? We can bring those days back." The hidden message is that you'll be happy again if you follow the speaker's advice.

- **Snob appeals.** The speaker tries to appeal to your pride. "Of course, most smart people like you think. . . ." Well, maybe they do—and maybe they don't.

- **Incite a riot.** The speaker uses language that's guaranteed to appeal to emotion, racism, or fear. Fear can be used to convince scared people.

- **Magic words.** Ad writers and politicians know that people respond to certain words. Words like "new and improved" and "this great country" get the audience on its feet every time.

Did you know?

The tiniest things can have a huge impact on history. In the 7th century, the T'ang cavalry in China began using long stirrups that allowed riders to stand while their horses galloped. It was such an improvement that the T'ang cavalry took over most of central China.

Testing for the Truth

When you read anything—from a textbook to a newspaper—use your critical thinking skills. Critical thinking is particularly important in social studies. People's values and experiences influence the way they view events. Being an active reader can help you dig out the truth. How do you do this?

In World
War II, the
Americans had a secret
weapon—the Navajo lang-
uage. It was used as the code
to send secret messages. The
code was never broken.

- **First, scan the reading.** Look for the author's point of view about the subject.

- **What do you know about the author?** For example, letters to the editor about recycling would be quite different written by a conservationist and by a manufacturer of bottles.

- **Watch for loaded words.** A writer who wants to throw doubt on someone might write, "Betty claimed she told the truth." That leaves a doubt in the reader's mind about whether Betty really did tell the truth.

- **Use what you know.** Compare what you know with the facts the author uses.

- **Does the writer present both sides of the issue?** If so, are both sides presented fairly? If not, look for bias.

Are You Primary or Secondary?

You'll find both primary and secondary sources when you research. What's the difference?

- A **primary source** is information about an event told by someone who experienced the event or an object that was made at the time of the event. A newspaper is a primary source. A television show or recording of an interview from the time is also a primary source. A photograph is a primary source.

- A **secondary source**, on the other hand, was created by someone who was not present at the time of the event. A book that a historian writes about the past is a secondary source. So is an encyclopedia.

Researchers use primary sources if they can because the information is not so far removed from the event. If you can, use primary sources in your research. But remember that everyone has a point of view that influences the way he or she sees events. This can be reflected in the details chosen, the angle of the photo, or the writer's opinion. Don't rely on only one source.

"Learn your history. Take the time and effort to find out who you are. "
—Denzel Washington,
actor

Three Ways to Think About Social Studies Essays

If you're writing an essay for a social studies class, here are some ways to organize it, in addition to presenting main points and supporting information.

- **Chronologically.** Often, events are most easily linked by tracing them in the order in which they happened. When you organize an essay chronologically, or in time order, simply begin at the beginning and tell what happened, one important event at a time. Make sure you have a theme that connects these events.

- **Cause and effect.** Sometimes it's a good idea to link ideas by cause and effect because one event influenced later events. When you're writing about the causes of a certain war or the importance of a particular event, this is a good structure to use.

- **Compare and contrast.** This structure works when you're discussing how things have changed over time. It also works when you're comparing how two events, places, or people differ and how they are similar.

Chart It? No, Graph It.

You're not quite sure how to use charts and graphs? It's a skill students of social studies often need. If you want to brush up on your graphing skills, see "Getting the Most from Graphs and Tables" on pages 113–115. The skills of interpreting graphs and charts will be useful to you in many classes. Many newspapers and magazines also use graphs and charts both to add interest and to show numbers in an exciting way.

George Washington would not let anyone publish a biography of him. Mason Locke Weems got around this rule by publishing after Washington died. It was Weems who invented the story of the cherry tree and "I cannot tell a lie."

Quiz

Are You Map Wise?

Understanding maps is important in social studies. Are you map wise? Take this quiz. If you need a map checkup, read on.

1. Do you know what the legend is on a map?
2. Do you know what a scale is?
3. Do you know the difference between a political map and a resource map?
4. Can you find your way using a topographical map?
5. Can you find latitude and longitude on a map?

The Key to Understanding Maps

Maps are designed for specific purposes. Basically, there are two kinds of maps: general maps and theme maps. A *general map* shows geographic information and locates places and features. A *theme map* shows a certain kind of information. A highway map, which focuses on roads that help travelers get from here to there, is a theme map.

Here is a guide to the main features of general maps. Notice the *inset*, or box, at the bottom of the map. It tells you what area you're seeing and gives you a key to the symbols used on the map. Also notice the *compass rose*, which shows you direction.

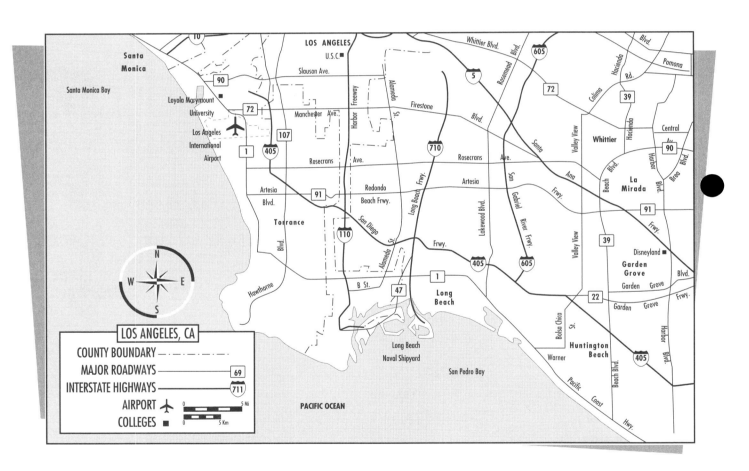

Latitude and Longitude

The imaginary lines that criss-cross maps and globes and help you locate places are called *latitude* and *longitude* lines.

Parallels measure latitude. Latitude is the distance in degrees north and south of the equator. The equator is located at 0 degrees and is midway between the north and south poles. There are 90 degrees of latitude north of the equator and 90 degrees of latitude south of the equator. All parallels are about 70 miles apart. The letter *N* or *S* tells you whether the latitude is north or south of the equator.

Meridians measure longitude. Longitude is the distance in degrees east and west of the prime meridian, which is located at 0 degrees longitude. The prime meridian passes through Greenwich, England, a suburb of London. Longitude lines run north and south on the globe. Unlike latitude lines, longitude lines are not parallel. They meet at the poles. The letter *E* or *W* tells you whether the longitude is east or west of the prime meridian.

Here's a visual guide to using latitude and longitude on a map.

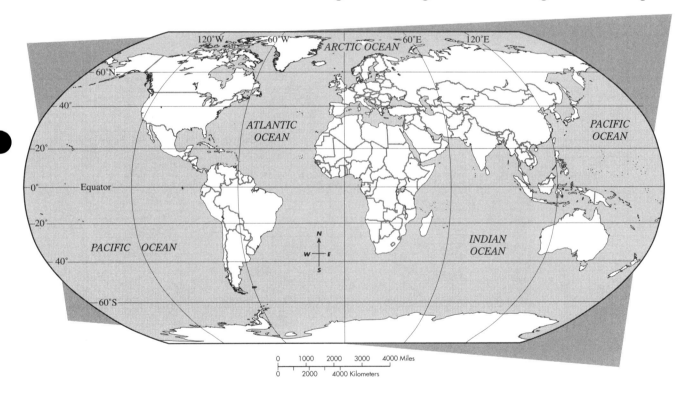

Specialized Maps

You will probably read many maps with many different kinds of information in social studies classes. If you understand how to use a legend and how to determine scale, though, you can read almost any map. Here are a few of the theme maps you are likely to see in social studies.

Political Maps. Political maps show the boundaries of governments. These may be counties, states, countries, and other kinds of divisions. The smaller the area the map covers, the smaller the governmental division.

Keeping up with the changes in the world can be a challenge for mapmakers. Make sure you use an up-to-date map in your research. If you were looking for Czechoslovakia, for example, you'd have a problem because the country no longer exists.

Here's an example of a political map.

Rainfall Maps. Rainfall maps show the average amount of rain that falls in an area. It is usually shown in inches, and as the average amount for a year.

Topographic Maps. Mapmakers use aerial photos to show how the land looks. They then make topographic maps by using tiny lines to show three dimensions. The general rule is that the closer together the lines are, the steeper the incline is.

Population Maps. Population maps show where people live and how many people live in an area. This is called the area's population density. Notice the key in the lower-left corner. It tells you that the areas on the map that are darkest are the areas in which the population density is greatest.

Here's an example of a population map.

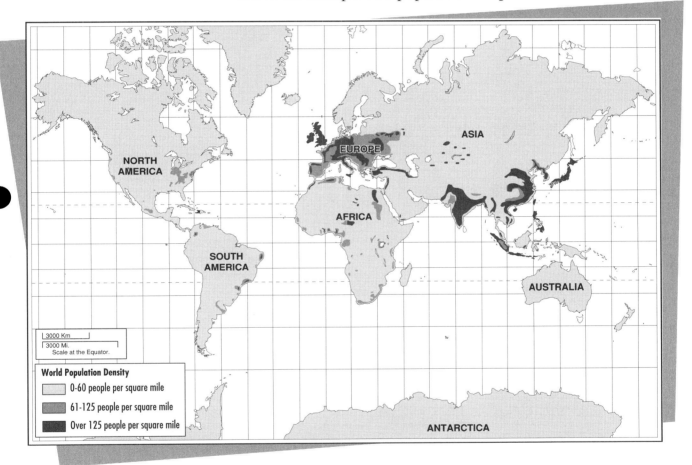

Resource and Product Maps. Resource and product maps show an area's mineral and other wealth and what products are produced there.

The resource map on the next page shows you the natural resources of Africa. Notice that the inset in the lower-left corner shows you the meaning of each of the map's symbols.

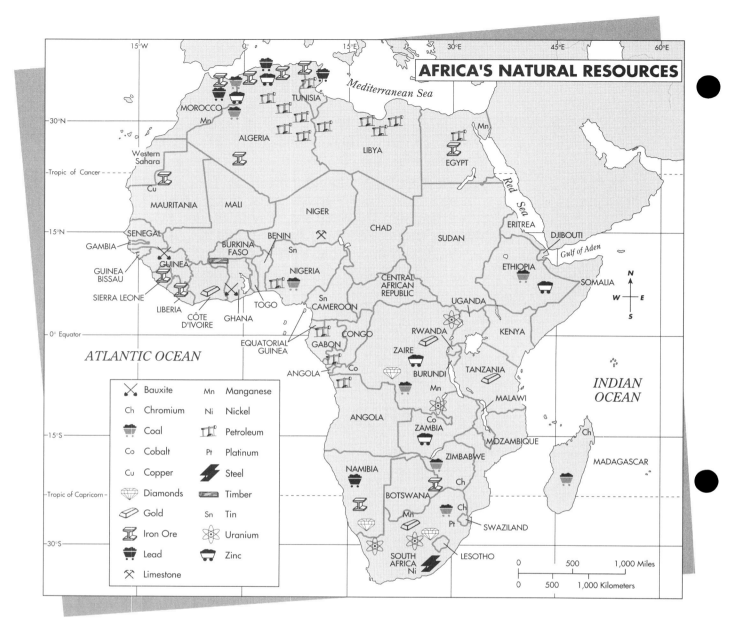

AFRICA'S NATURAL RESOURCES

Putting Maps Together

When you put maps together, you can often better understand the relationships between the information on different maps. For example, if you looked at population, rainfall, and product maps of the United States, you could guess that there are connections between where people live, what the rainfall is, and what produce people grow.

Maps can help you to see how people and areas relate to one another. Knowing how to read them can help you sail through social studies.

CHAPTER CHECKUP

Which of these tips do you use when you study social studies? Give yourself 1 point for each one you use.

✓ Use visual aids, such as maps, to keep track of the area you're studying.

✓ Ask yourself what the writer of your textbook or your teacher wants you to learn from the lesson.

✓ Think about social studies as a reporter does and ask yourself the Five W questions.

✓ Read biographies, watch documentaries, and find other sources to add to your social studies knowledge.

✓ Watch for propaganda when you read books and magazines and listen to people speak.

✓ Use active reading skills to tell opinion from fact.

✓ Know the difference between primary and secondary sources.

✓ Know three ways to organize social studies essays.

✓ Understand different kinds of maps, their uses, and how to read them.

✓ Understand how to locate places using latitude and longitude.

If your score is 8 or higher, you're going strong. If your score is below 8, review this chapter. You might also ask a friend, your study group, or your teacher for some tips that they use.

Now think about what you learned in this chapter.

1. Describe a documentary you've seen in school or at home. What was the subject of the documentary? What did you learn about the subject?

2. How can learning about propaganda help you become a wise consumer—and voter?

After You Read

Congratulations! You've just completed *Globe Fearon Survival Guide for Students*. Before you put this book down, there are a few things you should know.

First, don't put this book in an out-of-the-way place. Think of it as a reference book. Use it any time you're unsure of what your next step should be. You may refer to it the next time you are assigned a long-term project. Or maybe you'll need it to help you study for a math test. In any case, you'll find that *Globe Fearon Survival Guide for Students* is an invaluable tool—one that can help you again and again.

Second, remember that *Globe Fearon Survival Guide for Students* has two features designed to help you find the topics you need—the Table of Contents and the Index. For example, if you develop writer's block, you can look in either the Table of Contents or the Index to find sections that deal with this annoying subject.

In addition, the Table of Contents is arranged to give you an outline of the steps you'll need to take to complete a task. It can help you.

You may feel as if you need a general tune-up on your study skills. This is another opportunity for you to use the Table of Contents. Just look for the area that's giving you trouble and review the suggestions in that section. Both the Table of Contents and the Index will help you find the information you need in seconds.

Third, *Globe Fearon Survival Guide for Students* has a Reference section. This section has information that will help you achieve success in language arts, math, science, and social studies. It has a list of commonly misspelled words, a table of geometric shapes and formulas, the Periodic Table of the Elements, a list of the presidents of the United States, maps, and much more. There is even an Internet page. The Internet sites listed will give you a quick-start on finding what you need on the Net. You'll find that the Reference section is a great tool to keep handy.

Just remember, study skills are life skills. You can use the skills and techniques you've learned in *Globe Fearon Survival Guide for Students* at school and at work, now and in the future.

What Have You Learned?

Now that you have completed *Globe Fearon Survival Guide for Students*, answer the following questions to see how your study habits have changed. Remember, answer these questions honestly. You won't be graded on your answers. This quiz is for *you*.

Unit 1: Organizing Your Time and Your Life

1. Do you use to-do lists and master lists to help you prioritize your activities? (Chapter 1)
2. Do you write all of the things you have to do in an assignment calendar? (Chapter 2)

Unit 2: The Skills You Need to Succeed in School

3. Do you use your study style to help you learn? (Chapter 3)
4. Do you use your time in class to listen carefully, ask questions, and take useful notes? (Chapter 4)
5. Do you read actively? (Chapter 5)
6. Can you find the resources you need in the library? on the Internet? (Chapter 6)
7. Do you feel confident when you take tests? (Chapter 7)
8. Do you have a clear picture of your audience before you begin to write a paper? (Chapter 8)
9. Do you know how to complete all of the steps of writing a research paper? (Chapter 9)
10. Do you feel confident preparing for and giving a speech? (Chapter 10)

Unit 3: Studying in the Subject Areas

11. Do you know the major elements of fiction? the minor elements? (Chapter 11)
12. Do you use mental math to quick-check math problems? (Chapter 12)
13. Do you know how to read and interpret different kinds of graphs? (Chapter 13)
14. Do you easily read and interpret maps? (Chapter 14)

If you answered *yes* to all of these questions, you are on your way to becoming a successful student. If you answered *sometimes* or *no* to some questions, don't be discouraged. Work on changing your study habits—one at a time. Then use your study skills in all of your classes, and in your life. *Globe Fearon Survival Guide for Students* will help you form the skills you need to do your best work.

Language Arts

Commonly Misused Words

accept/except
 accept—to take or receive something
 except—to leave out
Please accept my invitation to the party.
I'll take all of the apples, except this one.

affect/effect
 affect—to have influence on
 effect—to cause something to happen
The medicine did not affect his cold.
The bad weather had an effect on the garden.

all ready/already
 all ready—prepared
 already—previously
We were all ready to go.
He had already gone.

buy/bye/by
 buy—to purchase
 bye—good-bye
 by—near or beside
How many apples can you buy for one dollar?
He left without saying bye.
She sat by the tree.

for/ four
 for—on the side of
 four—the number "4"
They fought for equality.
Her mom brought four shirts with her.

hear/here
 hear—to listen
 here—at or in this place
Can you hear me from next door?
Are they here yet?

it's/its
 it's—it is
 its—belonging to "it"
It's going to be cold tonight.
Put everything in its place.

knew/new
 knew—to have understood
 new—recent
I knew the answer to the problem.
She read the new sports magazine.

know/no
 know—to understand
 no—not at all
Do they know how to find the gym?
I have no money.

piece/peace
 piece—part of a whole
 peace—free from fighting
Can I have a piece of pie?
Someday there will be world peace.

than/then
 than—instead of
 then—after
I'd rather go to the movies than play basketball.
Do your chores. Then you can go out with
your friends.

their/there/they're
 their—belonging to "them"
 there—at or in that place
 they're—they are
The children put on their pajamas.
There are two oranges on the table.
They're earlier than they usually are.

through/threw
 through—by way of
 threw—tossed
He went through the woods to get to school.
She threw the football to her friend.

to/too/two
 to—toward
 too—also
 two—the number "2"
She went to the airport.
Did you buy this dress, too?
They bought two new bathing suits.

were/we're
 were—past tense of "to be"
 we're—we are
They were afraid of the dark.
We're going to the field hockey game
tomorrow.

your/you're
 your—belonging to "you"
 you're—you are
Is that your hat?
You're a really good friend.

Commonly Misspelled Words

accommodate	concentrate	government	maintenance	publicly	supersede
acknowledge	condemn	friend	miscellaneous	purpose	suspicious
acquaintance	conscience	fulfill	mischievous	questionnaire	technique
actually	conscious	grammar	Mississippi	receive	thief
aggravate	controversial	half	necessary	recommend	thieves
aisle	convenience	halves	neither	relevant	thorough
all right	courageous	harass	ninety	remembrance	through
analysis	cousin	height	noticeable	resemblance	tomorrow
announcement	criticism	heroes	nuclear	restaurant	tragedy
approximately	dependent	humorous	nuisance	rhythm	Tuesday
association	descendant	hygiene	occurrence	Saturday	twelfth
attendance	difference	ignorant	parallel	secretary	unanimous
audience	dissatisfied	illiterate	parliament	self, selves	undoubtedly
beginning	eighth	indefinitely	perseverance	separate	unnecessarily
benefited	embarrass	inevitable	persistence	siege	vacuum
brilliant	especially	interference	picnicking	significance	variety
bureaucracy	exaggerate	interpret	playwright	similar	various
changeable	except	irrelevant	potatoes	sincerely	vengeance
column	exciting	language	practically	situation	Wednesday
commitment	existence	license	privilege	squirrel	weird
committee	February	literature	psychology	stubbornness	weren't

Basic Spelling Rules

1. Use **i** before **e** except after **c**, or when **e** and **i** together sound like the letter **a** as in *neighbor* and *weigh*.

Examples:	field	chief	relief
	receive	deceive	reign

2. For some words ending in **-f** or **-fe**, change the **-f** or **-fe** to **-ve** before adding an **-s** to form the plural.

Examples:	half	halves
	knife	knives

3. When the singular form of a word ends in **-s**, **-c**, **-ch**, **-sh**, or **-z**, add the letters **-es** to form the plural.

Examples:	branch	branches
	tax	taxes

4. When words end in **-ce** or **-ge**, keep the **e** before suffixes **-able** and **-ous**.

Examples:	notice	noticeable
	outrage	outrageous

5. When verbs end in **-ie**, change the **-ie** to **-y** before adding **-ing**.

Examples:	lie	lying
	tie	tying

6. When verbs in the present tense end in **-y**, change the **-y** to **-ied** to form the past tense.

Examples:	study	studied
	dirty	dirtied

Basic Punctuation Rules

1. a. Use a **period** at the end of a sentence that is not a question or an exclamation.
   Examples: He likes ice cream. Please shut the door.
   b. Use a **period** after abbreviations.
   Examples: Mrs., Ms., Dr., U.S., N.Y.

2. Use a **question mark** to end a question.
   Examples: Where are you? Do you like baseball?

3. Use an **exclamation point** to end a strong expression of feeling.
   Examples: I hate this T-shirt! I don't believe they did that!

4. Use a **comma** to separate words and phrases in a series.
   Example: He likes chicken, fish, and hamburgers. She went out into the cold, dark, snowy night.

5. Use a **semicolon** to take the place of a conjunction (and, or, but). Remember that both halves of the sentence should be able to stand alone.
   Example: The boat was in poor shape; it could not float.

6. Use a **colon** to introduce a list.
   Examples: Four people were there: Derrell, Kathleen, Marilyn, and Ryan.

7. Use an **apostrophe** to show possession or to indicate a contraction.
   Examples: Shouldn't we go in Mimi's car?

8. Use **quotation marks** around a direct quotation.
   Example: You said, "Don't take it."

Eight Parts of Speech

1. A **noun** refers to a person, place, thing, object, or idea. A **common** noun refers to any person, place, thing, object, or idea.
   Examples: boy, city
   A **proper noun** is capitalized and refers to a particular person, place, thing, object, or idea.
   Examples: Keith, Boston

2. A **pronoun** takes the place of a noun.
   Example: The dog buried *his* bone and *he* couldn't find *it*.

3. A **verb** shows action or a state of being.
   Examples: He *called* his friend. (action)
   She *is* here. (state of being)

4. An **adjective** describes nouns and pronouns.
   Examples: The *little, red* wheelbarrow
   She likes *chocolate* ice cream.

5. An **adverb** describes verbs, adjectives, or other adverbs.
   Examples: The child ran *quickly*.
   Ice is *really* cold.

6. A **preposition** shows the relationships between nouns, pronouns, and other words.
   Examples: Apollo 11 landed *on* the moon.
   Milk is stored *inside* a refrigerator.

7. A **conjunction** joins words or groups of words.
   Examples: Yesterday I relaxed *and* read a book.
   She did well on the test *because* she studied.

8. An **interjection** shows strong emotion and is usually followed by an exclamation point.
   Examples: *No!* I refuse to go with you!
   Wow! How beautiful!

Common Irregular Verbs

Present Tense	Past Tense	Past Particple
be	was, were	been
become	became	become
begin	began	begun
break	broke	broken
bring	brought	brought
catch	caught	caught
choose	chose	chosen
come	came	come
do	did	done
draw	drew	drawn
drive	drove	driven
eat	ate	eaten
fall	fell	fallen
feed	fed	fed
feel	felt	felt
find	found	found
fly	flew	flown
get	got	gotten, got
give	gave	given
go	went	gone
have	had	had
hear	heard	heard
keep	kept	kept
know	knew	known
leave	led	led
make	made	made
prove	proved	proved, proven
read	read	read
ride	rode	ridden
ring	rang	rung
run	ran	run
say	said	said
see	saw	seen
send	sent	sent
sing	sang	sung
take	took	taken
teach	taught	taught
tear	tore	torn
throw	threw	thrown
wear	wore	worn
write	wrote	written

Editing Marks

Move text — Tyra went the to mall.

Delete — I have ~~have~~ no money.

Insert — Dwayne is throwing a surprise party for Wayne.

No space — Joe likes to play basketball.

Add period — Alan fell off his skateboard.

Add apostrophe — Its been a long time since I've seen Juan.

Add comma — Jim, Rasheed and Patrick scored touchdowns.

Add quotation marks — Sarah said, My dog ate my homework.

Lowercase — Malik went to a Supermarket to buy eggs.

Capitalize — I would love to visit Puerto rico.

Begin paragraph — Finally, I would like to thank my teammates for their dedication.

Math

Geometic Shapes and Formulas

l	length	*r*	radius
w	width	a^2	"a" squared
h	height	π	pie = 3.14

Circumference of a circle = $2\pi r$

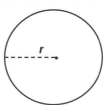

Area of a triangle = $\dfrac{\text{base} \times \text{height}}{2}$

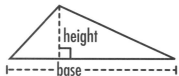

Perimeter of a rectangle = 2 × (*l* + *w*)
Area of a rectangle = *l* × *w*

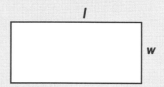

Volume of a cube = *l* × *w* × *h*

Volume of a cylinder = 2π × *r* × (*r* + *h*)

Two complementary angles add up to 90°

Two supplementary angles add up to 180°

Pythagorean theorem = $a^2 + b^2 = c^2$

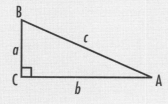

Mathematical Symbols

+	plus
−	minus
x	times
÷	divided by
=	equals
<	less than
>	greater than
≤	less than or equal to
≥	greater than or equal to
^{2}	squared
$\sqrt[2]{}$	square root of
≈	approximately

Algebra/Factoring

$$(a - b)^2 = a^2 - 2ab + b^2$$
$$(a + b)^2 = a^2 + 2ab + b^2$$
$$(a - b)(a + b) = a^2 - b^2$$
$$(a + b)(c + d) = ac + ad + bc + bd$$
$$(a + b)(a + c) = a^2 + ac + ab + bc$$

Commutative property of addition
$$a + b = b + a$$

Commutative property of multiplication
$$ab = ba$$

Associative property of addition
$$a + (b + c) = (a + b) + c$$

Associative property of multiplication
$$a(bc) = (ab)c$$

Distributive property of multiplication over addition
$$a(b + c) = ab + ac$$

Distributive property of multiplication over subtraction
$$a(b - c) = ab - ac$$

Fractions, Decimals, and Percents

1	=	1.0	=	100%
3/4	=	0.75	=	75%
2/3	=	$0.\overline{666}$	=	66.6%
1/2	=	0.5	=	50%
1/3	=	$0.\overline{333}$	=	33.3%
1/4	=	0.25	=	25%
1/5	=	0.2	=	20%
1/6	=	0.16	=	16.6%
1/7	=	0.142	=	14.2%
1/8	=	0.125	=	12.5%
1/9	=	$0.\overline{111}$	=	11.1%
1/10	=	0.1	=	10%

Fractions

$\dfrac{3}{5}$ — numerator
— denominator

Addition and subtraction:
first find a common denominator, then add or subtract

$$\frac{1}{2} + \frac{3}{8} = \frac{4}{8} + \frac{3}{8} = \frac{7}{8}$$

Multiplication:
multiply the numerators, and multiply the denominators

$$\frac{1}{3} \times \frac{2}{3} = \frac{1 \times 2}{3 \times 3} = \frac{2}{9}$$

Division: multiply the first fraction with the reciprocal of the second fraction

$$\frac{3}{12} \div \frac{1}{4} = \frac{3}{12} \times \frac{4}{1} = \frac{12}{12} = 1$$

Squares and Square Roots

n	n²	√n
1	1	1
2	4	1.414
3	9	1.732
4	16	2
5	25	2.236
6	36	2.449
7	49	2.646
8	64	2.828
9	81	3
10	100	3.162
11	121	3.317
12	144	3.464

Temperature

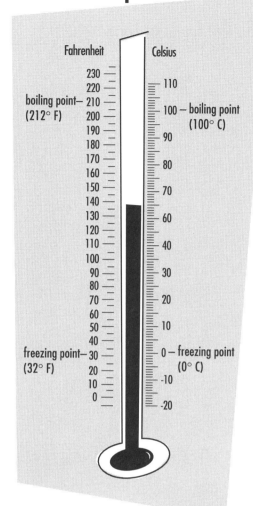

Order of Operations

1. Do operations within parentheses. ( )

2. Do powers and roots. $\sqrt[2]{}$

3. Do multiplication and division in order from left to right. × ÷

4. Do addition and subtraction in order from left to right. + −

See the numbered steps in this example.

$$3^2 \quad × \quad (2+3) \quad + \quad (4 × 5) \quad = \quad 65$$

1		5	20	
2	9			
3	9	×	5	
4	45		+ 20	= 65

Roman Numerals

I	1	X	10	D	500
V	5	L	50	M	1,000
		C	100		

I	1	V	5	IX	9	XCVI	96
II	2	VI	6	X	10	DLXIX	569
III	3	VII	7	XXIV	24	MCMXCVIII	1998
IV	4	VIII	8	XLVII	47	MMX	2010

English System

1 foot (ft)	=	12 inches (in)
1 yard (yd)	=	3 feet = 36 inches
1 mile (mi)	=	1,760 yards = 5,280 feet
1 tablespoon (T)	=	3 teaspoons (t)
1 cup (c)	=	16 T = 8 fluid ounces (fl oz)
1 pint (pt)	=	2 c
1 quart (qt)	=	2 pt = 4 c = 32 fl oz
1 gallon (gal)	=	4 qt
1 ft^2	=	144 in^2
1 yd^2	=	9 ft^2
1 acre	=	4,840 yd^2

Metric System

1,000 (kilos)	100 (hectas)	10 (decas)	1	1 (decis)	.01 (centis)	.001 (millis)
km	hm	dam	m	dm	cm	mm
kg	hg	dag	g	dg	cg	mg
kl	hl	dal	l	dl	cl	ml

m	=	meter
g	=	gram
l	=	liter
1 m^2	=	10,000 cm^2
1 hectare (ha)	=	10,0000 m^2
1 km^2	=	100 ha

Multiplication Table

	1	2	3	4	5	6	7	8	9	10	11	12
1	1	2	3	4	5	6	7	8	9	10	11	12
2	2	4	6	8	10	12	14	16	18	20	22	24
3	3	6	9	12	15	18	21	24	27	30	33	36
4	4	8	12	16	20	24	28	32	36	40	44	48
5	5	10	15	20	25	30	35	40	45	50	55	60
6	6	12	18	24	30	36	42	48	54	60	66	72
7	7	14	21	28	35	42	49	56	63	70	77	84
8	8	16	24	32	40	48	56	64	72	80	88	96
9	9	18	27	36	45	54	63	72	81	90	99	108
10	10	20	30	40	50	60	70	80	90	100	110	120
11	11	22	33	44	55	66	77	88	99	110	121	132
12	12	24	36	48	60	72	84	96	108	120	132	144

Science

Scientific Method

1. Identify and state the problem.
Scientists often state the problem as a question.

2. Gather information.
Scientists read about work that has already been done.

3. State a hypothesis.
Scientists clearly state what they expect to find out in their experiment.

4. Design an experiment.
Scientists design an experiment to test their hypothesis.

5. Make observations and record data.
Scientists observe their experiment and carefully record data.

6. Organize and analyze data.
Scientists organize their data into charts and graphs and analyze this data.

7. State a conclusion.
Scientists state whether the data supports their hypothesis.

Geological Time Line

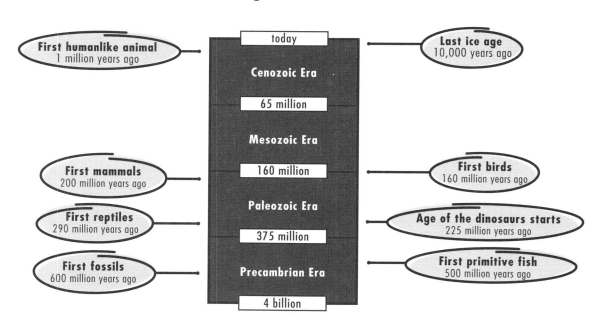

Nutrition Pyramid

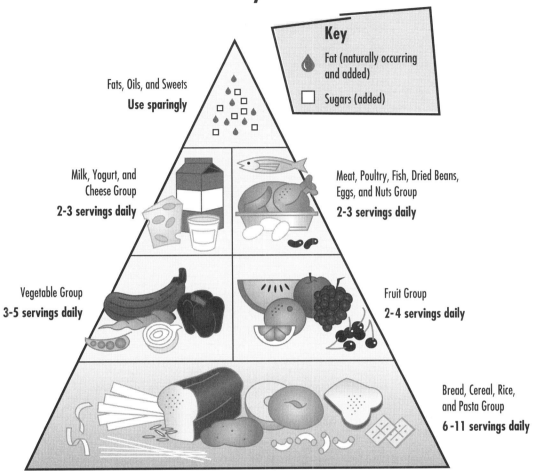

Key

💧 Fat (naturally occurring and added)

☐ Sugars (added)

Fats, Oils, and Sweets
Use sparingly

Milk, Yogurt, and Cheese Group
2-3 servings daily

Meat, Poultry, Fish, Dried Beans, Eggs, and Nuts Group
2-3 servings daily

Vegetable Group
3-5 servings daily

Fruit Group
2-4 servings daily

Bread, Cereal, Rice, and Pasta Group
6-11 servings daily

Classification of Organisms

CLASSIFICATION	HUMAN BEINGS	LEOPARD FROG	COMMON STARLING
Kingdom	Animalia	Animalia	Animalia
Phylum	Chordata	Chordata	Chordata
Class	Mammalia	Amphibia	Aves
Order	Primate	Anura	Passeriformes
Family	Hominidae	Ranidae	Sturnidae
Genus	Homo	Rana	Sturnus
Species	sapien	pipiens	vulgaris

KEY:

1.01
H
1

1.01 — mass number, A
H — symbol
1 — atomic number, Z

1	2	3	4	5	6	7	8	9	10	11	12	13	14	15	16	17	18
1.008 H 1																	4.003 He 2
6.94 Li 3	9.012 Be 4											10.81 B 5	12.01 C 6	14.01 N 7	16.00 O 8	19.00 F 9	20.17 Ne 10
22.99 Na 11	24.31 Mg 12											26.98 Al 13	28.09 Si 14	30.97 P 15	32.06 S 16	35.45 Cl 17	39.95 Ar 18
39.10 K 19	40.08 Ca 20	44.96 Sc 21	47.90 Ti 22	50.94 V 23	52.00 Cr 24	54.94 Mn 25	55.85 Fe 26	58.93 Co 27	58.71 Ni 28	63.55 Cu 29	65.38 Zn 30	69.72 Ga 31	72.59 Ge 32	74.92 As 33	78.96 Se 34	79.90 Br 35	83.80 Kr 36
85.47 Rb 37	87.62 Sr 38	88.91 Y 39	91.22 Zr 40	92.91 Nb 41	95.94 Mo 42	98.91 Tc 43	101.1 Ru 44	102.9 Rh 45	106.4 Pd 46	107.9 Ag 47	112.4 Cd 48	114.8 In 49	118.7 Sn 50	121.8 Sb 51	127.6 Te 52	126.9 I 53	131.3 Xe 54
132.9 Cs 55	137.3 Ba 56	138.9 ★La 57	178.5 Hf 72	180.9 Ta 73	183.9 W 74	186.2 Re 75	190.2 Os 76	192.2 Ir 77	195.1 Pt 78	197.0 Au 79	200.6 Hg 80	204.4 Tl 81	207.2 Pb 82	209.0 Bi 83	(209) Po 84	(210) At 85	(222) Rn 86
(223) Fr 87	226.0 Ra 88	227 •Ac 89	(261) Rf 104	(262) Ha 105	(263) Sg 106	(262) Ns 107	(265) Hs 108	(266) Mt 109	(272) Unn 110								

★ Lanthanoid Series

140.1 Ce 58	140.9 Pr 59	144.2 Nd 60	145 Pm 61	150.4 Sm 62	152.0 Eu 63	157.3 Gd 64	158.9 Tb 65	162.5 Dy 66	164.9 Ho 67	167.3 Er 68	168.9 Tm 69	173.0 Yb 70	175.0 Lu 71

• Actinoid Series

232.0 Th 90	231.0 Pa 91	238.0 U 92	237.0 Np 93	244 Pu 94	243 Am 95	247 Cm 96	247 Bk 97	251 Cf 98	254 Es 99	257 Fm 100	258 Md 101	259 No 102	260 Lr 103

Social Studies

Presidents and Vice Presidents of the United States of America

President	Vice President	Years in Office	President	Vice President	Years in Office
1. George Washington	John Adams	1789–1797	23. Benjamin Harrison	Levi P. Morton	1889–1893
2. John Adams	Thomas Jefferson	1797–1801	24. Grover Cleveland	Adlai E. Stevenson	1893–1897
3. Thomas Jefferson	Aaron Burr George Clinton	1801–1805 1805–1809	25. William McKinley	Garret A. Hobart Theodore Roosevelt	1897–1901 1901–1901
4. James Madison	George Clinton Elbridge Gerry	1809–1813 1813–1817	26. Theodore Roosevelt	 Charles W. Fairbanks	1901–1905 1905–1909
5. James Monroe	Daniel D. Tompkins	1817–1825	27. William H. Taft	James S. Sherman	1909–1913
6. John Quincy Adams	John C. Calhoun	1825–1829	28. Woodrow Wilson	Thomas R. Marshall	1913–1921
7. Andrew Jackson	John C. Calhoun Martin Van Buren	1829–1833 1833–1837	29. Warren G. Harding	Calvin Coolidge	1921–1923
8. Martin Van Buren	Richard M. Johnson	1837–1841	30. Calvin Coolidge	 Charles G. Dawes	1923–1925 1925–1929
9. William Henry Harrison	John Tyler	1841–1841	31. Herbert C. Hoover	Charles Curtis	1929–1933
10. John Tyler		1841–1845	32. Franklin D. Roosevelt	John N. Garner Henry A. Wallace Harry S Truman	1933–1941 1941–1945 1945–1945
11. James K. Polk	George M. Dallas	1845–1849			
12. Zachary Taylor	Millard Fillmore	1849–1850	33. Harry S Truman	 Alben W. Barkley	1945–1949 1949–1953
13. Millard Fillmore		1850–1853			
14. Franklin Pierce	William R. King	1853–1857	34. Dwight D. Eisenhower	Richard M. Nixon	1953–1961
15. James Buchanan	John C. Breckinridge	1857–1861	35. John F. Kennedy	Lyndon B. Johnson	1961–1963
16. Abraham Lincoln	Hannibal Hamlin Andrew Johnson	1861–1865 1865–1865	36. Lyndon B. Johnson	 Hubert H. Humphrey	1963–1965 1965–1969
17. Andrew Johnson		1865–1869	37. Richard M. Nixon	Spiro T. Agnew Gerald R. Ford	1969–1973 1973–1974
18. Ulysses S. Grant	Schuyler Colfax Henry Wilson	1869–1873 1873–1877	38. Gerald R. Ford	Nelson A. Rockefeller	1974–1977
19. Rutherford B. Hayes	William A. Wheeler	1877–1881	39. James E. Carter	Walter F. Mondale	1977–1981
20. James A. Garfield	Chester A. Arthur	1881–1881	40. Ronald Reagan	George Bush	1981–1989
21. Chester A. Arthur		1881–1885	41. George Bush	J. Danforth Quayle	1989–1993
22. Grover Cleveland	Thomas A. Hendricks	1885–1889	42. William Clinton	Albert Gore, Jr.	1993–

States of the United States

State	Abbreviation	Capital	Date of Admission	State	Abbreviation	Capital	Date of Admission
Alabama	AL	Montgomery	1819	Montana	MT	Helena	1889
Alaska	AK	Juneau	1959	Nebraska	NE	Lincoln	1867
Arizona	AZ	Phoenix	1912	Nevada	NV	Carson City	1864
Arkansas	AR	Little Rock	1836	New Hampshire	NH	Concord	1788
California	CA	Sacramento	1850	New Jersey	NJ	Trenton	1787
Colorado	CO	Denver	1876	New Mexico	NM	Santa Fe	1912
Connecticut	CT	Hartford	1788	New York	NY	Albany	1788
Delaware	DE	Dover	1787	North Carolina	NC	Raleigh	1789
Florida	FL	Tallahassee	1845	North Dakota	ND	Bismarck	1889
Georgia	GA	Atlanta	1788	Ohio	OH	Columbus	1803
Hawaii	HI	Honolulu	1959	Oklahoma	OK	Oklahoma City	1907
Idaho	ID	Boise	1890	Oregon	OR	Salem	1859
Illinois	IL	Springfield	1818	Pennsylvania	PA	Harrisburg	1787
Indiana	IN	Indianapolis	1816	Rhode Island	RI	Providence	1790
Iowa	IA	Des Moines	1846	South Carolina	SC	Columbia	1788
Kansas	KS	Topeka	1861	South Dakota	SD	Pierre	1889
Kentucky	KY	Frankfort	1792	Tennessee	TN	Nashville	1796
Louisiana	LA	Baton Rouge	1812	Texas	TX	Austin	1845
Maine	ME	Augusta	1820	Utah	UT	Salt Lake City	1896
Maryland	MD	Annapolis	1788	Vermont	VT	Montpelier	1791
Massachusetts	MA	Boston	1788	Virginia	VA	Richmond	1788
Michigan	MI	Lansing	1837	Washington	WA	Olympia	1889
Minnesota	MN	St. Paul	1858	West Virginia	WV	Charleston	1863
Mississippi	MS	Jackson	1817	Wisconsin	WI	Madison	1848
Missouri	MO	Jefferson City	1821	Wyoming	WY	Cheyenne	1890

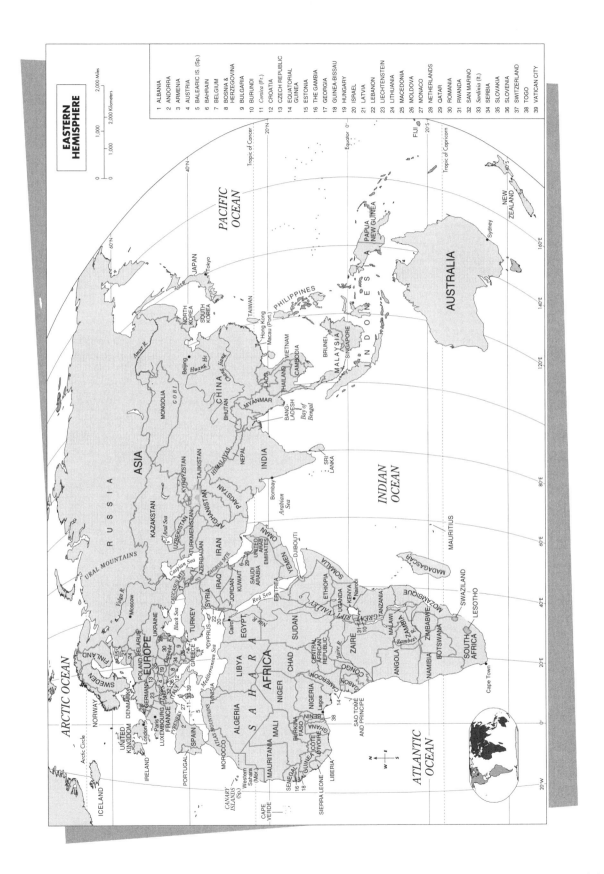

EASTERN
HEMISPHERE

1	ALBANIA
2	ANDORRA
3	ARMENIA
4	AUSTRIA
5	BALEARIC IS. (Sp.)
6	BAHRAIN
7	BELGIUM
8	BOSNIA & HERZEGOVINA
9	BULGARIA
10	BURUNDI
11	Corsica (Fr.)
12	CROATIA
13	CZECH REPUBLIC
14	EQUATORIAL GUINEA
15	ESTONIA
16	THE GAMBIA
17	GEORGIA
18	GUINEA-BISSAU
19	HUNGARY
20	ISRAEL
21	LATVIA
22	LEBANON
23	LIECHTENSTEIN
24	LITHUANIA
25	MACEDONIA
26	MOLDOVA
27	MONACO
28	NETHERLANDS
29	QATAR
30	ROMANIA
31	RWANDA
32	SAN MARINO
33	Sardinia (It.)
34	SERBIA
35	SLOVAKIA
36	SLOVENIA
37	SWITZERLAND
38	TOGO
39	VATICAN CITY

ARCTIC OCEAN

Bering Strait

Beaufort Sea

Alaska (U.S.)

Greenland (Den.)

Baffin Bay

Hudson Bay

Labrador Sea

CANADA

CANADIAN SHIELD

NORTH AMERICA

Vancouver

Montreal

St. Lawrence R.

Great Lakes

ROCKY MTS.

Great Salt Lake

UNITED STATES

APPALACHIAN MTS.

Mississippi R.

Los Angeles

ATLANTIC OCEAN

Tropic of Cancer

Hawaii (U.S.)

Rio Grande

MEXICO

Gulf of Mexico

BAHAMAS

HAITI

DOMINICAN REPUBLIC

CUBA

Puerto Rico (U.S.)

Mexico City

BELIZE

ANTIGUA & BARBUDA

JAMAICA

Caribbean Sea

ST. VINCENT & THE GRENADINES

DOMINICA

BARBADOS

PACIFIC OCEAN

GUATEMALA

EL SALVADOR

HONDURAS

NICARAGUA

COSTA RICA

PANAMA

TRINIDAD AND TOBAGO

Caracas

GUYANA

SURINAME

VENEZUELA

French Guiana (Fr.)

COLOMBIA

Equator

ECUADOR

AMAZON BASIN

Amazon R.

PERU

SOUTH AMERICA

BRAZIL

ANDES

Lima

São Francisco R.

WESTERN HEMISPHERE

Lake Titicaca

BOLIVIA

Tropic of Capricorn

PARAGUAY

20°S

CHILE

ARGENTINA

PAMPAS

URUGUAY

Buenos Aires

0   500   1,000 Miles

0   500   1,000 Kilometers

PATAGONIA

40°S

160°W   140°W   120°W   100°W   80°W   60°W   40°W   20°W

80°N

Arctic Circle

40°N

20°N

0°

Internet

Language Arts Sites

Links for Writer's Resources

http://www.vmedia.com/shannon/writing.html

* Experiencing writer's block? This web site is a list of further writers' resources for you to check out. Links include the following and more:
~ General Writing Help   ~ Genre Writers' Resources
~ Reference Manuals   ~ Writers' Associations &
~ Professions Related   Listings
   to Writing   ~ Fun Stuff

Web Poetry Kit

http://www.best.com/~jnc/cd/poetrykit.html

* Submit your poetry for publication on the web.

Inkspot

http://www.inkspot.com/

* Need a break from writing a paper? This site is a virtual library of links to a variety of writer resource web pages. Links include the following and more:
~ Writers' Classified Ads   ~ How To Get Published
~ Articles & Interviews   ~ Site For Young Writers
~ Workshops   ~ Further Links

A Celebration of Women Writers

http://www.cs.cmu.edu/People/mmbt/women/writers.html

* Explore the writing of female authors from around the world. You can be linked to actual online text by the author you've chosen.

Math and Science Sites

MacTutor History of Mathematics Archive

http://www-groups.dcs.st-and.ac.uk:80/~history/

* Check out the historical side of mathematics and the individuals who shaped the field. You can explore the following and more:
~ Biography Index   ~ History Topic Index
~ Famous Curves Index   ~ Birthplace Map
~ Chronologies

Eisenhower National Clearinghouse (ENC)

http://www.enc.org/

* What's new in the fields of mathematics and science? Check out links to the following sites and more:
~ Directed math—"how to"   ~ Further Resources
~ Puzzles

Exploring Math and Science

http://explorer.scrtec.org/explorer/aux/webed/wEdlist.html

* Are you an explorer? This site looks at the fields of math and science in a fun and interesting way. It contains links to the following sites and more:
~ Mathematics   ~ Science
~ The Environment   ~ Further Links

Mega Mathematics

http://www.c3.lanl.gov/mega-math/

* Want to try some interesting math activities? This site asks you to examine real-life problems and find mathematical solutions to them. Links include the following and more:

~ Mathematical Vocabulary   ~ Further Resources

~ Puzzles

The Franklin Institute Science Museum

http://sln.fi.edu

* Check out the exciting interactive science exhibits at the Franklin Institute in Philadelphia, PA, and more:

~ Tour Online Exhibits   ~ Science Student Resources

~ Science News and Activities

NASA (The National Aeronautics and Space Administration)

http://www.gsfc.nasa.gov/NASA_homepage.html

* Blast off with the official homepage for NASA. This site offers you links to past and present projects that NASA has conducted.

Social Studies Sites

The Smithsonian

http://www.si.edu/newstart.htm

* If you've never been to the Smithsonian Institution in Washington, D. C., now is your chance. This site has links to all of the Smithsonian museums as well as many other valuable sites on the Web.

The White House

http://www.whitehouse.gov/WH/Welcome.html

* Explore the official home page for the White House. This site gives you the opportunity to contact government officials and examine issues that the White House is currently facing.

Recreation Hall

http://www.voicenet.com/~acasas/rechall/rechall.html

* Need a primary source? This site helps you explore various cultures and texts. Links include the following and more:

~ Newspapers   ~ Texts Online

~ Online Documents   ~ Recordings Of

~ Explorations On   Famous Speeches

    Historical Cultures   ~ Further Links

History Buffs Homepage

http://www.historybuff.com

* Are you a history buff? This site will give you information on newspaper printing and publishing history and U. S. history in general. Links include the following and more:

~ Searchable Libraries   ~ History Bulletin Board

~ History Resources   ~ Further Links

INDEX